WHAT WE OWE

WHAT WE OWE

*Truths, Myths, and Lies
about Public Debt*

CARLO COTTARELLI

BROOKINGS INSTITUTION PRESS
Washington, D.C.

The Brookings Institution is a private nonprofit organization devoted to research, education, and publication on important issues of domestic and foreign policy. Its principal purpose is to bring the highest quality independent research and analysis to bear on current and emerging policy problems. Interpretations or conclusions in Brookings publications should be understood to be solely those of the authors.

Library of Congress Cataloging-in-Publication data are available.
ISBN 978-0-8157-3067-5 (cloth : alk. paper)
ISBN 978-0-8157-3069-9 (ebook)

9 8 7 6 5 4 3 2 1

Typeset in Minion

Composition by Westchester Publishing Services

There is a limit to the time assigned you,
and if you don't use it to free yourself
it will be gone and never return.

MARCUS AURELIUS

I am the king of debt.
I love debt.

DONALD TRUMP

Contents

PART III
The Main Road

WHAT WE OWE

Introduction

The April 26, 2016, cover of *Time* magazine told Americans, in no uncertain terms, that they had a problem, and a big one: each one of them, "every American man, woman and child," would have to pay $42,998.12 to erase the $13.9 billion U.S. debt. The lead article, "The United States of Insolvency," by James Grant, sent equally worrisome messages: the path of federal debt is unsustainable, debt cannot keep rising, at one point it will stop rising, and that will happen "when the world loses confidence in the dollars we owe."

Public debt has indeed surged in the last ten years in the United States, as well as in many other advanced economies. Indeed, in the aftermath of the 2008 global economic and financial crisis—the deepest since the 1930s—the rise in public debt in most other advanced economies was unprecedented, because it occurred in peacetime. Over the last two to three centuries (and probably also before), all major surges in public debt were caused by wars. Not this time: public debt surged in the absence of a major war and now stands at historical levels in most advanced countries. In only a few cases has it started to decline.

And yet, despite the alarming *Time* cover, not too many seem to be worried about public debt. In the United States, the public debt issue did not feature prominently in the 2016 presidential campaign, and now President Donald Trump's planned tax cuts to stimulate the economy will be financed, at least in the immediate future, by borrowing more. In Japan, the country with the highest level of public debt in the world, Abenomics, the set of economic policies named after the country's prime minister, Shinzō Abe, continues to feature repeated bouts of fiscal stimulus. And in most European countries, people and policymakers seem to be more worried about the austerity packages needed to rein in public debt than about the consequences of high debt.

And, after all, why should people worry? Granted, some European countries—Greece, Portugal, Ireland, Cyprus—did suffer public debt crises during 2010–12, but many saw this more as the result of the incomplete features of the euro zone's economic and monetary institutional architecture than as the effect of excessive debt accumulation. Moreover, if too much public debt is a problem, why are interest rates on public debt so low? Interest rates on government paper in most advanced economies have started to edge up but are still quite low by historical standards. And why exactly is public debt harmful? How big does public debt have to be before it starts hurting the economy? Most important, if public debt is the problem, what is the solution?

These are just some of the puzzles concerning public debt. They are difficult to solve, for two reasons. First, economics is not an exact science, and matters relating to public debt are among the most difficult ones to tackle. Second, those matters are often perceived as having deep political implications: government debt is like no other debt because it emerges from public spending and taxation decisions and hence reflects the role of the government in an economy. These political implications are not very conducive to an objective discussion of problems related to public debt. Consequently, positions are often just stated rather than argued: on one side, anti-austerity advocates refuse to consider the risks arising from high public debt; on the other side, public debt is demonized, without proponents even bothering to explain what the consequences would be of letting the public debt grow, or of not bringing it down.

This book tries to bring some clarity to the subject of public debt: what it is, why it can be harmful, and when it can be harmful. The book, however, is not just about the disease (to the extent that public debt is a disease). Indeed, most of it deals with the remedies, their benefits, and their undesirable side effects, as well as the circumstances under which one remedy should be preferred to others. The focus is on advanced economies, which experienced the largest increase in public debt since 2007, but much of the discussion could also apply to emerging economies.

I have tried to write an honest book, unpolluted by political considerations. The book is also honest in another sense: it does not pretend that all the puzzles can be easily solved. Yet it does contain some tentative (at least personal) conclusions. Here the reader will find some good news and some bad. The bad news: if left unattended, high public debt can indeed harm economic growth, if not through overt debt crises, at least by lowering long-term growth prospects. The good news: lowering public debt will take time, but as long as we recognize that there is a problem and we act in time, bringing down public debt will not require traumatic solutions. It can be done through a moderate degree of fiscal adjustment (a moderate degree of austerity that would not be inconsistent with continuing growth) combined with structural reforms to boost growth to the extent possible. As long as we act in time, as I said. . . .

Understanding the book does not require any particular knowledge of economics, but I hope the chapters might be of interest also to those who are familiar with economic thinking. The simplicity of the language does not detract from analytical rigor.

The book owes much to my former colleagues at the International Monetary Fund, particularly those in the Fiscal Affairs Department, which I headed from October 2008 to October 2013. I would also like to thank Antonio Spilimbergo and two anonymous referees for helpful comments. Finally, my thanks go to Antonio Bassanetti, Roberto Basso, Maria Cannata, Floriana Cerniglia, Valeria Miceli, Simonetta Nardin, Andrea Presbitero, and Michalis Psalidopoulos for comments on an earlier version of this book, published in Italy in 2016.

The royalties from the sale of this book will be donated to UNICEF.

Part I

THE PUBLIC DEBT PROBLEM

ONE

What Is Public Debt?

Public debt—the total of the nation's debts; debts of local and state and national governments; an indicator of how much public spending is financed by borrowing instead of taxation.

—Definition of public debt from www.webster-dictionary.org

L et's start with the basics: what is public debt, and where does it come from? If you already know the basics, you can jump to chapter 2, but it may still be worth reading the last two sections of this chapter, "Money and Public Debt" and "The Missing Debt."

The Basics: Government Deficit, Government Surplus, and Public Debt

Never trust those who tell you that a government's budget is like a household's budget. In many respects it is not. And yet similarities in some basic aspects do emerge. So, let's think about your own household. Your annual income is $60,000, but you need to spend $70,000. How do you bridge the $10,000 difference? You borrow from your bank at an interest rate of 5 percent, to be paid next year. If you start your year with zero debt, by the end of the year your debt will be $10,000. Next year, nothing changes, except that your expenses rise from $70,000 to $70,500 as you must pay the bank $500 for interest on your debt. Your bank, however, is generous and not only rolls over the initial debt but lends you another $10,500 to cover your new imbalance between your revenues and your spending. At the end of the second year, your debt has reached $20,500.

Let's now introduce some terms that economists use to talk about government finances. The imbalance between the government spending and its revenues (in the above household example, $10,000 in the first year and $10,500 in the second year) is called the *government, or fiscal, deficit.* The amount the government owes at the end of the year is the *public,* or sometimes *government* or *national, debt* (in the example above, $10,000 after one year and $20,500 after two years). It grows because the government has a deficit. Indeed, broadly speaking, public debt is the cumulative sum of all previous deficits.[1] Debt can go down in terms of dollars, or of whatever national currency, only if, in a given year, government revenues exceed government spending, in which case the government, instead of running a deficit, is running a surplus. So public debt goes up when there is a deficit and comes down when there is a surplus. If revenues and spending are equal, the government is running a balanced budget and the debt goes neither up nor down.

One last definition: the *primary deficit* is the deficit net of interest payments. In the above household example, it is $10,000 in the first year as well as in the second year. It is unchanged because the amount of spending excluding interest payments (what economists call *primary spending*) does not change. This says that your deficit can go up even if your revenues and primary spending do not change. It goes up because interest payments accumulate and keep rising as long as debt rises, as credit card holders know very well.

In modern times, governments, unlike households, do not typically borrow from banks. They borrow by selling securities to investors. The securities with a maturity of up to one year are often called *Treasury bills,* while other securities are referred to as *government bonds,* or take fancier names according to their specific features, for example, whether their yield is fixed or indexed to short-term interest rates or inflation. All these securities are sold primarily through auctions, and the yield that each security bears depends on the result of the auction: so whereas a household can negotiate the interest rate on a loan with a bank, the yield of government debt is determined by the interaction of many investors through the auction mechanism.

One additional complication is that almost every country has different levels of government. At one extreme are local governments, such as municipalities, while at the other there is a central government or, in federal nations such as the United States, a federal government. In between are regional or state governments. All these entities may run deficits and borrow, mostly by issuing securities but, especially in the case of municipalities, also by borrowing from banks. Sometimes these government entities even hold securities issued by other government entities (a situation common for social security administrations, which often buy paper issued by the central government). In most of this book the term "public debt" will be used to refer to what has been borrowed by all these central and local administrations, often referred to as *general government*, usually net of the debt held by components of the general government itself.[2]

Some Features of Government Debt That May Affect Its Riskiness and Yield

In advanced economies, government securities are often regarded as the quintessential risk-free asset and therefore are able to offer much lower interest rates than securities issued by the private sector. Lending to the government is regarded as quite safe because the government has the power to raise revenues by taxing people. Private borrowers cannot do this, and therefore lending to them is riskier. Indeed, many have argued that public debt is desirable precisely because economies need a steady supply of risk-free assets, whereby investors can hold the assets with a low yield but also at no risk. Some may remember that in the 1990s, many were worried that the stream of budgetary surpluses that characterized the Clinton administration would deprive America, and the whole world, of a supply of risk-free assets.

But are government securities really risk-free? Raising taxes does not win elections, so one should have doubts about the willingness of governments to raise revenues to repay debt under any circumstances. And indeed, in economic history, hundreds of cases of governments defaulting on their debt can be found. So let's now look at some of the factors that affect the risk that the government will not repay you and, therefore, the yield (the *risk premium*) investors will request when they lend to the government (we return to this issue in more depth in chapter 3).

First, the size of public debt is certainly relevant: the larger the size of public debt, the higher the tax revenues needed to service it, and thus the more the government will be tempted to declare bankruptcy. To understand the risk associated with public debt, however, just looking at the level of debt in terms of dollars, euros, or pounds is not sufficient. The risk associated with a certain amount of debt also depends on the amount of national resources that could potentially be taxed. A good proxy for these resources is given by a country's gross domestic product (GDP), or what a nation produces every year, as most government revenues come from the taxation of GDP or its components (consumption spending, for example). That is why economists usually look at public debt as a percentage of GDP. This is not a neutral choice, though. For example, since 2007 the rise in public debt has been very strong in terms of percentage of GDP but much less strong in terms of percentage of private sector wealth, or at least financial sector wealth. But, as mentioned, taxes on GDP are the main source of government revenue. Moreover, GDP data are more easily available than data on wealth, and it is by now common practice to focus on the public debt-to-GDP ratio as a key indicator of the riskiness of public debt. Of course, looking at public debt-to-GDP ratios rather than at debt expressed in national currency also makes it easier to compare levels of debt across countries and over time.

In addition to its size, four other features of public debt may affect its riskiness. The first one is the composition of those who buy government securities, and in particular, whether investors are domestic or foreign residents. If debt is held primarily by foreigners, the risk that the government will be unable to roll over its debt is higher because foreigners are often the first to run if there are doubts about the government's willingness to repay its debt. Moreover, the temptation to repudiate public debt is stronger if investors are foreigners: first, they do not vote, and second, if investors are predominantly foreigners, the negative impact of debt repudiation on the national economy is smaller (more on this in chapter 10). Another important issue relating to the composition of the investors has to do with the share of securities held by the central bank. We return to this topic in the next section.

The second feature of government debt that affects its riskiness is its average maturity. Some securities are to be repaid in a few months, some in two years, others in twenty-five years' time or longer. Economists often look at the average residual life of government securities, or sometimes to a similar concept, called *duration*.[3] For a given amount of debt, the shorter the average residual life, the greater is the amount of securities that will mature every month and that will have to be rolled over—in more technical terms, the higher is the government's *gross borrowing requirement* (the total amount of securities that must be sold, or the sum of what needs to be rolled over and what is needed to finance the new deficit). In turn, the larger the gross borrowing requirement, the higher is the potential pressure that could arise in the government paper market should investors start doubting the government's willingness to repay its debt. The perceived risks would be correspondingly stronger.[4]

The third key feature of government debt affecting its riskiness relates to its currency denomination. A country can issue securities denominated in its own currency, as the United States does, or in the currency of another nation. For example, many developing countries issue securities denominated in U.S. dollars, euros, or Japanese yen, because they believe they can more easily attract investors this way. The currency denomination strongly affects the risks associated with public debt. But to understand how this happens, it is important to focus on a fourth key aspect of the composition of public debt, one that relates to the interaction between the government and its central bank and to how, directly or indirectly, the government can finance its deficit by borrowing from outside the public sector or by printing money. This is a key issue for the riskiness of public debt, as well as for its macroeconomic effects.

Money and Public Debt

Modern states have the ability to create money from nothing, or at least just from paper and ink. They usually do not do it directly but through each country's central bank: for example, the Federal Reserve in the United States, the Bank of England in the United Kingdom, and the European Central Bank for euro-zone countries. Four things must be understood about printing money.

The first one is obvious: printing money is profitable. Printing pieces of paper costs very little, but with money you can buy things or you can lend money and earn interest. The beauty of it is that people who need money for their transactions are happy to receive those useless pieces of paper in payment for the goods and services they provide. Economists have coined a name for the profit arising from printing money: *seigniorage.* We return to this concept later in the book.

Second, even if the money is printed by the central bank, it is the government that benefits from the bulk of seigniorage, because central bank profits, even when the central bank is not legally owned by the government, are typically returned to the government.

Third, and relatedly, when the government borrows from the central bank—that is, when the central bank buys government paper either directly from the government or indirectly from the market—that part of borrowing does not cost the government anything: the interest paid by the government to its central bank is returned to the government when the profits of the central bank are transferred to it. This makes a big difference: if the government finances its deficit by issuing securities on the market, it needs to make interest payments and to worry about rolling over the securities when they come to maturity. If the government finances its deficit by borrowing from its central bank, it does not need to worry about all this.

Fourth, in today's world, central banks create money not just by printing banknotes; they also create electronic money. For example, when they buy a government security from a commercial bank, they pay by crediting the account of the commercial bank at the central bank. That is also money, although in electronic form. Whatever we say about money applies not only to banknotes but also to electronic money. It is easier, however, to think in terms of banknotes, so you do not need to worry about this additional complication.

If financing the fiscal deficit by printing money is so good for the government, why then does the government not finance itself just by printing money? The reason is that by abusing its power to print money, the government can kill the goose that laid the golden eggs. People are willing to use money issued by the government for their transactions because they have confidence that those pieces of paper will maintain their value over time. But if too many of those pieces of paper are floating around, and people realize that they are going to be flooded with pieces of paper because the government has a huge deficit to finance, they will lose confidence in the value of money and try to get rid of it as soon as they receive it by buying things. This drives up the prices of goods and services, as well as asset prices, and ultimately could even lead to a switch to a different currency. This happened in Ecuador, which abandoned its currency in 2000 and is completely "dollarized," having fully substituted the U.S. dollar for its own currency. More generally, the main episodes of hyperinflation in history, including Germany's post–World War I inflation, have all been linked to abuse by the government of its power to print money. And even before banknotes were introduced, one popular option for sovereigns short of cash, including some prominent Roman emperors, starting with Nero, was to reduce the gold or silver content of coins while maintaining their face value.

We come back to this issue in chapter 7, in a discussion of whether printing money could be the solution to high public debt. For the moment, I would just underscore something quite surprising regarding public debt statistics. While economics textbooks are clear about the difference between financing deficits by borrowing from the private sector and by printing money, public debt statistics, including those discussed in the next chapter, do not really make this distinction. Public debt data include both the money that has been borrowed from private investors and that which has been borrowed from the central bank—although, as discussed, this is not really "borrowing" because the interest the government pays is returned to it when central bank profits are passed to the government.

There is a formal reason for this anomaly: from an accounting point of view, the money borrowed from the central bank is formally a liability and so it is part of the debt definition. But there is perhaps a more substantive reason: if we believe that a surge in the amount of borrowing from the central bank, matched by a surge in money in circulation, can only be temporary, to avoid the risk of killing the goose that laid the golden eggs, then it may be preferable to keep track of total government debt, including the debt held by the central bank, which will eventually have to be replaced by regular borrowing. But there are different views on this, as will be discussed in chapter 7.

Let's return to the issue we started with: the need to distinguish whether the government has borrowed in domestic currency or in foreign currency. It does make a difference. If the government has borrowed in domestic currency, the debt may be repaid by printing money (there may be institutional barriers to overcome, but technically it is possible). Inflation may result, but the government may deem this preferable to, for example, having to default on its debt. If instead the government has borrowed in foreign currency, and it cannot print it to repay its debt, there is a higher risk that the government will be unable to pay. This scenario is described by some economists, starting with Barry Eichengreen and Ricardo Hausmann in 1999, as the "original sin" of many emerging markets that borrowed in foreign currency and were later unable to repay their debt.

In virtually all advanced economies, the bulk of public debt is denominated in national currency. However, euro-zone countries, while having a debt denominated in their own currency, do not individually have access to central bank resources because there is a common central bank, the European Central Bank, which does not take orders from any of its member countries individually. This feature has complicated the management of the 2011–12 European debt crisis, and the provision of adequate liquidity financing to the euro zone, thus also contributing to the view that European countries would be better off if they left the euro zone (see chapter 8).

The Missing Debt: Derivatives and Pension Debt

Two important items are not usually included in the standard definition of public debt. The first involves some technical details and is not so important for the rest of this book, but the second one comes up in chapter 2, so focusing on it is recommended.[5]

The first is the debt that arises from derivative contracts the government has signed with financial institutions, usually banks. These contracts typically imply that the government must pay or receive money from the counterparty bank, depending on certain developments in financial markets, such as whether interest rates rise or fall. Governments enter into these contracts to reduce the effect of financial sector developments on the cost of their debt. For example, if interest rates on public debt rise, the government will have to make higher interest payments on its debt. A derivative contract ensures that, if interest rates do rise, the government will receive a partial compensation from the counterparty bank. The downside of this mechanism is that if instead interest rates decline, the government will have to make payments, which reduces the benefits that would be realized when interest rates fall. Every month, as interest rates move up or down, the government either receives payments or makes payments as a result of outstanding derivative contracts. At any moment the market value of these derivative contracts (the "debt" arising from them, in case future payments prevail) is equal to the sum of future payments (more precisely, the net present value of those payments) the government will have to make, based on prevailing market interest rates at various maturities. Therefore, this value changes over time as interest rates change. The figures involved are usually not huge but not trivial either. In the case of Italy, a country that has actively engaged in derivative operations, this form of debt amounted to 2.6 percent of GDP at the end of 2014, a relatively small figure compared to Italy's greater than 130 percent of GDP recorded public debt. However, the fact that, as a result of derivative contracts, the government may have to pay banks sizable amounts of money is often the source of much political controversy. Those in charge of public debt management may be accused of having bet and lost public money out of incompetence or worse. In reality, there is nothing fundamentally wrong with these operations: they are just like an insurance against bad events, such as a rise in interest rates. Of course, if those events do not materialize, or if circumstances turn out to be even more favorable than expected (an interest rate decline), there is a price to pay, in the same way that there is a price to pay for a regular insurance contract, namely, the insurance premium.

The second form of unrecorded debt is social security (or "pension") debt, by far the most important one in terms of size, including in the United States, where, as we will see in chapter 2, it is quite large. Pension debt is related to the payments that the government through its social security institutions must make in the future as a result of existing pension legislation and rules. There are various definitions of pension debt. For example, some countries, while not adding pension debt to the standard debt definition, publish statistics, at least for public sector employees, on the present value (the sum, discounted by some interest rate) of pension payments that have already accrued, even if they are not yet payable because those employees have not yet retired. I prefer to use a definition of pension debt that is more closely linked to pressures that may arise in the future on the fiscal accounts and that are not already captured by today's fiscal deficit and debt figures. In particular, my former colleagues in the Fiscal Affairs Department of the International Monetary Fund developed and publish annually in the IMF's *Fiscal Monitor*, for several countries, the net present value of future increases in pension spending-to-GDP ratios over the next thirty-five to forty years. It is useful to look at these increases in pension spending because social security revenues are likely to rise in line with GDP as social security contributions are, broadly speaking, a fixed percentage of earnings. Thus, looking at the increases in pension spending with respect to GDP provides an estimate of the increasing (or decreasing) imbalance in the accounts of the social security system and the fiscal account in general. As discussed in the next chapter, pension debt computed in this way can be very large: in some countries it is equivalent to a large share of, even as large as, official public debt. It cannot therefore be forgotten even if it does not give rise to the potentially more pressing problems associated with financial debt, notably the risk of a rollover crisis.

TWO

The Surge in Public Debt

There are 10^{11} stars in the galaxy. That used to be a huge number.
But it's only a hundred billion. It's less than the national deficit!
We used to call them astronomical numbers. Now we should call
them economical numbers.

—Richard Feynman

I t's time to look at some numbers. This chapter focuses on the surge in
public debt that advanced economies experienced in the aftermath of the
2008–09 global economic and financial crisis and, more generally, on the
status of public finances in these countries, from a historical perspective.

The Surge

Developments in the public finances of most advanced economies since
2007 were unprecedented. Public debt-to-GDP ratios started rising at a
speed that had never been experienced in the absence of major wars. This
anomaly is well described in figure 2-1, which depicts the average of public
debt ratios across major advanced economies (the G-7, consisting of the
United States, Japan, Germany, the United Kingdom, France, Italy, and
Canada) since the end of the nineteenth century.

Two major surges in the public debt ratio were recorded in history before the most recent one, on the occasions of the two world wars. These surges reflected the acceleration in military spending that wars require and that is typically financed by borrowing rather than by raising taxes.[1] A smaller increase in the average public debt ratio was observed in the early 1930s as a result of the Great Depression. When GDP declines, public deficits rise because government revenues fall and some spending, for example for unemployment benefits, rises. Larger deficits mean a faster accumulation of public debt. Moreover, the debt-to-GDP ratio is also directly boosted by a decline in GDP (the denominator of the ratio). During the Great Depression these forces raised the average public debt ratio of advanced economies by about twenty percentage points. The 2008–09 recession, however, caused a much larger surge in the public debt ratio. Public debt in the G-7 countries increased by over forty percentage points of GDP between the end of 2007 and the end of 2016, even if the decline in GDP was much more contained than the one experienced in the early 1930s (indeed, by 2011 GDP had recovered to its 2007 level for the aggregate of these economies). The reason for this faster and more prolonged rise in public debt was that fiscal policy was used much more actively than in the 1930s to support economic activity. As income initially fell, and revenues declined, deficits were allowed to increase. Moreover, additional measures were introduced to increase public spending and reduce tax rates in support of economic activity. Finally, although this is not the main reason for the surge in public debt in most countries, public money was used to support banks in trouble.[2]

This more intense fiscal policy activism was by and large appropriate, and indeed is one of the reasons why the 2008–09 crisis ended up involving smaller output losses than the Great Depression. But the side effect was a larger amount of accumulated public debt.

One additional problem is that the surge in public debt after 2007 had been preceded by a prolonged period of upward creep in public debt ratios starting in the mid-1970s. This gradual rise brought the average public debt ratio in the G-7 countries from some 40 percent of GDP in the mid-1970s to more than 80 percent in 2007. The increase reflected various forces coming to bear, primarily higher spending for health care and social security programs that was only partly matched by increases in taxation (or was matched only with a delay). The starting point for the final jump up was therefore

FIGURE 2-1. Advanced Economies: Public
Debt-to-GDP Ratio, 1880–2015

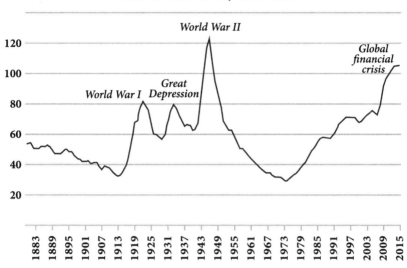

Source: S. Ali Abbas and others, "A Historical Public Debt Database," Working Paper 10/245 (Washington, D.C.: International Monetary Fund, November 2010) (www.imf.org/external/pubs/ft/wp/2010/wp10245.pdf).

already quite high in a historical perspective, and, as a result of the post-2007 surge, the debt ratio in 2016 reached a level that had only been exceeded, and then only briefly, in the aftermath of World War II.

Where Are We Now? A Cross-Country Snapshot

How do countries rank in this unpleasant public debt race? The year-end 2015 ranking, based on data published by the International Monetary Fund (IMF), is presented in figure 2-2. Leading all others is Japan, with an impressive debt-to-GDP ratio of some 250 percent of GDP, followed by a few countries whose debt problems have been at the center of the European fiscal policy debate over the past few years and often at the center of financial market attention: Greece, with a ratio of 183 percent of GDP, followed by Italy and Portugal, both at around 133 percent of GDP. Two more countries, the United States and Belgium, exceed the psychological

FIGURE 2-2. Public Debt-to-GDP Ratio, 2015

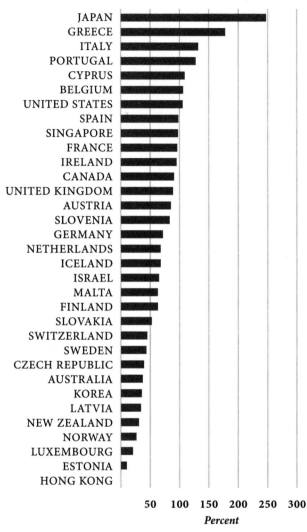

Source: IMF *Fiscal Monitor*, October 2016 (www.imf.org/en/Publications/FM/Issues /2016/12/31/Debt-Use-it-Wisely).

100 percent threshold (not really a benchmark for anything, but it is always interesting to see when you move from a two- to a three-digit debt figure).[3] A few more countries hover between 90 and 100 percent: Spain (also often under financial market pressure over the past few years), France, Cyprus (another country in trouble earlier in the 2010s), and Canada.

Just below 90 percent is the United Kingdom. At a much lower level is Germany, with a debt ratio below 70 percent of GDP, confirming the stereotype of fiscal conservatism that characterizes the largest euro-zone economy.

A small parenthetical comment on the United States: U.S. officials, and perhaps most U.S. economists, would say that the U.S. public debt is much smaller than the figure reported above. They would probably mention a figure of about 75 percent of GDP. This is the so-called public debt held by the public, which excludes intergovernmental holdings.[4] The figure for the United States reported in figure 2-2 also excludes intergovernmental holdings but is larger than 75 percent because it refers not only to the federal government (that is what in official U.S. statistics is meant by public debt) but also to the debt of subnational government entities, such as states and municipalities, in line with what is done for other countries. U.S. officials do not really like this definition and prefer to focus on the federal debt, arguing that the federal government is not responsible for the debt of states and municipalities. But focusing on federal government debt alone is misleading when debt is expressed as a ratio involving GDP, as GDP provides a revenue base not only for the federal government but also for municipalities and states. In other words, the federal government is not the only entity that can claim a slice of the GDP pie, so using the whole U.S. GDP to scale only one component of public debt does not seem right, and is especially misleading in making international comparisons. The bottom line is that the public debt-to-GDP ratio in the United States is much larger than the one reported by many.[5]

Let's go back to figure 2-2. The list of high-debt countries tells you something important: at the top of the ranking are many countries whose government paper market was under severe strain earlier in the 2010s. However, there are also high-debt countries, such as the United States and Japan, whose government paper continues to be regarded as a safe haven in times of market turmoil. This suggests that having a high debt level is a necessary but not a sufficient condition to get into trouble. Other things matter too, and we return to them later in the book.

One more thing should be noted. For some countries, the data reported in figure 2-2 do not tell the whole story. They are based on gross debt numbers and do not take into account the financial assets that a government may have. The holdings of financial assets are not irrelevant in evaluating the implications of a certain gross debt level. If a government has large financial assets, it can use the interest receipts on those assets to pay the interest due on its debt, with the result that in net terms, the debt service payment would be much smaller. Among the countries with high debt ratios that we considered above, looking at net debt is particularly important for Japan and Canada: net of financial assets held by the government, Japan's debt ratio, while remaining one of the highest, drops to about 130 percent of GDP, while Canada's debt ratio drops to less than 30 percent of GDP.[6]

That said, in most cases economists and market analysts prefer to focus on gross public debt as financial assets may bear a lower yield than government paper and may not be liquid enough to protect the government from rollover risks.[7]

Other Features of Government Debt That Shed Light on Cross-Country Differences

Let's now look at how countries fare in terms of some of the features of public debt that we highlighted in chapter 1 as being relevant in affecting the risk arising from high debt.

The first is the average residual life, or average maturity, of outstanding government securities. I can be brief here. With the exception of the United Kingdom, whose government paper has traditionally a very long maturity (almost fifteen years on average), the average maturity of all other major countries falls in the range of five to seven years, with the United States being on the lower side of this range at 5.7 years. Some smaller countries, such as Austria, Belgium, and especially Ireland, have longer average maturities.

More interesting differences arise with respect to the composition of investors and in particular the split between domestic and foreign residents, which is depicted in figure 2-3. Here the star performer is Japan, with as much as 90 percent of its public debt held by domestic residents. This is seen by many as the key reason why Japan has never experienced a government debt crisis despite having one of the highest public debt ratios in the world. Japanese households and financial institutions love holding securities issued by their government and they do not diversify much their asset portfolio. This provides stability to Japan's investor base (as long as Japanese investors do not start diversifying their portfolios; see chapter 3).

FIGURE 2-3. Holdings of Public Debt by Residents, 2015

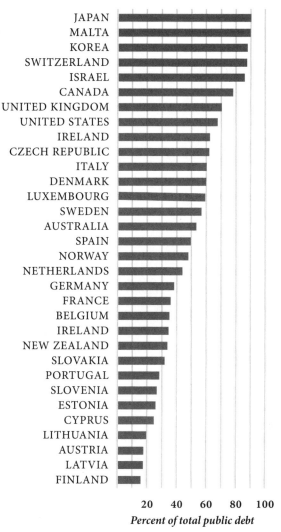

Percent of total public debt

Source: IMF *Fiscal Monitor*, October 2016 (www.imf.org/en/Publications/FM/Issues /2016/12/31/Debt-Use-it-Wisely).

Another interesting case is the United States. About two-thirds of its government securities are held domestically, including by its central bank, the Federal Reserve (the Fed). If we dig further, we see another important feature of the U.S. debt market. The bulk of U.S. government debt held abroad is held by the central banks of other countries—that is, not by private banks or individuals but by public institutions. The U.S. dollar is what economists call a *reserve currency*, that is, a currency in which the central banks of other countries hold their reserves. Actually, the U.S. dollar is the key reserve currency as the U.S. government paper market is highly liquid, and investing in it has traditionally been regarded, and continues to be regarded, as virtually risk-free, despite the recent surge in public debt. (We return to this topic in chapter 3.) For the moment it suffices to note that more than one-fifth of federal government securities, one-third of those held outside the general government sector, and two-thirds of those held abroad are held by foreign central banks, with the first and most important investor, just ahead of Japan, being China: by itself, China holds 6.5 percent of U.S. government debt. China's share started rising as China began recording larger and larger exports and surpluses in its trade with the rest of the world, including the United States. Essentially, this means that Chinese workers were producing computers and other merchandise for U.S. consumers and returned the money, via their central bank, to America by buying U.S. Treasury paper. The share of U.S. debt held by China was less than 1 percent in 1999, reached a peak of more than 8 percent in 2010, and declined slowly thereafter as China diversified its reserve portfolio. It remains quite high, though. That is perhaps not such great news from a geopolitical perspective, especially if the U.S. attitude toward China's trade policies toughens up.

Finally, let's look at pension debt. We saw in chapter 1 that this is a special form of debt, not something that needs to be rolled over every month in the market but something that will nonetheless put pressure on public finances over time. Pension debt has been on the rise for some time owing to population aging. As life expectancy increases, the liability for the public sector arising from public pensions also increases. The amount of pension debt as a percentage of GDP is reported in figure 2-4, as computed and projected by the IMF for 2016–50. Cross-country differences reflect differences in demographic forces (how fast societies are projected to age) and in features of the pension systems (for example, how rapidly, based on current legislation, the retirement age is projected to increase as the population ages). On top is Korea, whose pension debt is about twice as large as its financial debt. Pension debt is also high in the United States, Germany, New Zealand, and Belgium. It is low to negative (signaling a projected decline in pension spending over the next few decades) in countries that, while aging, have already reformed their pension system, such as Italy. Does high pension debt bring bad news for the countries affected? Yes, to

FIGURE 2-4. Pension Debt

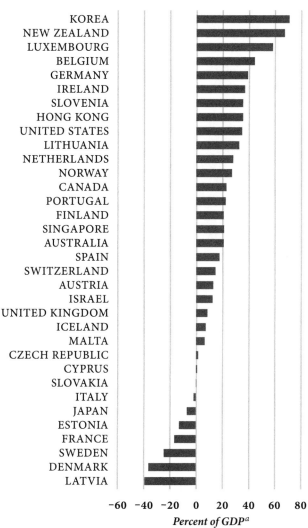

Source: IMF *Fiscal Monitor,* October 2016 (www.imf.org/en/Publications/FM/Issues /2016/12/31/Debt-Use-it-Wisely).

a. Net present value of increased spending for public pensions as projected for 2016–50.

some extent. High pension debt indicates that pressures on public spending will increase in the future, and those pressures will have to be faced. The good news is that the financial markets do not seem to be excessively worried about the existence of pension debt. Or, put differently, high pension debt is certainly viewed as an aggravating factor when financial debt is high, but I have not seen any country getting into trouble because pension debt is high when financial debt is low.

Before concluding this section, I will also mention another form of debt, similar to pension debt, that is frequently the focus of the fiscal policy debate in some countries, including the United States: the present value of future increases in public health care spending. The reason why I have so far resisted mentioning what we may call "health care debt" is that its estimates are much more uncertain than those of pension debt. They depend not only on demographics but also on technical progress in health care. Contrary to what many believe, the main driver of the large increases in health care spending over the past few decades has not been population aging but technical progress, namely, the availability of medical products that are much better than those that were available decades ago but are also much more expensive. Whether this situation will continue to obtain or whether technical progress might eventually lead to a decline in costs is uncertain, but the central projections made by experts imply that a decline in costs will not be realized. As a result, health care spending is projected to rise in most countries, leading to huge health care debt figures. While these estimates must be taken with a grain of salt, according to the IMF, health care debt is as high as 117 percent of GDP in the United States, the second largest after the Netherlands (where it is 122 percent of GDP).[8] The projected long-term surge in health care debt and pension debt is at the core of concerns about the viability of the current fiscal policy framework in the United States so often expressed by the Congressional Budget Office and the nonpartisan Committee for a Responsible Federal budget.[9] These international comparisons show that the United States faces greater hurdles from a cross-country perspective as well.

The Great Interest Rates Puzzle

Let's go back to the surge in gross public debt ratios. One of the most surprising things about this surge is that it occurred without causing a generalized rise in interest rates on government securities. One might have expected that, in order to induce investors to buy more government paper, the government would have had to pay higher interest rates: it is the law of demand and supply. However, interest rates on government paper declined in most countries while public debt increased.

For example, in 2007 the interest rate on U.S. ten-year bonds was 4.6 percent. By the end of 2015 it had dropped to 2.2 percent and it has continued to decline during most of 2016, edging up only recently (as new deficit-increasing measures were announced by the Trump administration). In Japan the yield on ten-year government bonds in 2007 was 1.7 percent. It is now virtually zero, after having been negative for some time. A large drop has also occurred in the euro zone: German interest rates fell from 4.3 percent in 2007 to little more than zero in 2016. Even in Italy, which has been subject to intense market pressure in some years, interest rates fell from 4.7 percent in 2007 to 1.5 percent in mid-2016, although they started rising in late 2016. How is this possible? Should investors not have asked for a higher interest rate to be willing to hold more government bonds in their portfolios and to take on the increased risk of not being repaid, given the higher indebtedness of sovereign borrowers?

One reason for the fall in interest rates could be the decline in inflation. What matters for investors is the purchasing power of the money they get when the loan is repaid with respect to the purchasing power of that money when the loan was granted (that is, the yield of the loan "in real terms"). If I lend $100 to the government and after one year I receive $103 (a 3 percent nominal interest rate), but in the meantime prices have increased by 1 percent, my real gain (the real interest rate) is only 2 percent, which is the nominal interest rate minus the inflation rate. (The actual formula for the real interest rate is slightly more complicated, but let's stick to this simple definition.) If inflation and inflation expectations decline, then the same real interest rate can be achieved with a lower nominal interest rate. So a decline in inflation and inflation expectations should cause a decline in interest rates. Inflation has declined significantly since 2007. For example, inflation was about 3 percent in 2006–07 and is now around 1.5–2 percent in most advanced economies. However, what should matter is the inflation that is expected over the lifetime of the government security that has been purchased, and according to most measures, inflation expectations have declined much less, so that real interest rates and not only nominal interest rates on government paper seem to have fallen, despite the surge in public debt.

Many factors could have influenced the decline in real interest rates on government paper, including the availability of increased savings to be invested in government paper in emerging economies such as China, where households save a large proportion of their income. Some influential economists, Larry Summers among them, believe we have entered an era in which real interest rates will be lower than in the past and could even be negative, which would make high public debt more sustainable over time.[10]

While all these factors may be relevant, I offer a much simpler solution to the higher public debt, lower interest rate puzzle: the decline in interest rates is likely to have been greatly affected by what central banks did in 2008 and after. Central banks started buying government paper in massive amounts. Indeed, the data on public debt that we have considered so far largely overestimate the actual increase in government paper that was sold to private investors.

Recall what was said in chapter 1: the government deficit can be financed either by borrowing from the private sector or by printing money, which in the modern world means by borrowing from your central bank. What has happened is that large shares of government deficits have been financed by central banks by printing banknotes and, especially, by electronic money, not by private investors.

The numbers are staggering, although not much quoted. Between year-end 2008, when central bank activism on the government paper market started in earnest, and year-end 2015, about one-third of the increase in public debt in the United States was purchased by the Fed. In other words, of the thirty-three percentage point increase in the public debt-to-GDP ratio that took place during that period, the actual increase in government securities held outside the central bank amounted to only about twenty-two percentage points of GDP. For the United Kingdom, the purchases of government securities by the Bank of England offset more than half the increase in the public debt-to-GDP ratio. The figures are even more impressive in Japan, where virtually all the increase in public debt was purchased by the Bank of Japan. Indeed, if we focus on the increase in Japan's net debt (as noted earlier, in Japan the government holds large amounts of financial assets), the purchases of government paper by the Bank of Japan largely exceeded the increase in net public debt, which probably means that the stock of public debt held by the private sector in Japan actually declined since 2008. In the euro zone the purchases of government paper by the European Central Bank (ECB) were not as large until recently. But they were still sizable, amounting to almost one-fourth the increase in the public debt ratio of the euro zone between 2008 and 2015. Moreover, the purchases accelerated sharply in 2016 as a result of the new program to increase the liquidity of the euro zone and raise inflation to a level closer to the ECB's inflation objective of "close to but below 2 percent." These large purchases also imply that the ranking of countries by their public debt-to-GDP ratio changes significantly if we exclude the debt held by central banks. For example, the net debt of the general government net of the purchases of government paper by central banks in Japan falls to just 71 percent of GDP at year-end 2015, pretty close to that of the United States (67 percent), the euro zone (64 percent), and the United Kingdom (61 percent).

These purchases of government securities by central banks were undertaken to support the economy by injecting liquidity, not to finance the government, which would be prohibited by the statute of many central banks, including the ECB.[11] But even if this was not the purpose, a major side effect was to facilitate the financing of government debt. Note that interest rates would tend to decline even if central banks injected money into the financial system by buying private sector securities or by lending to banks, but the effect on government bond yields is likely to be stronger if central banks buy government paper directly.

The impact of these purchases of government paper on the amount of money in the economy—more precisely, on the amount of what economists call the *monetary base*, that is, banknotes and the deposits of commercial banks at the central banks—has been huge. In the seven years from the end of 2008 to the end of 2015, the monetary base more than doubled in the United States and almost quadrupled in Japan and the United Kingdom. The increase in the euro zone was close to 50 percent, but again, there was a sharp acceleration during 2016.

In my view, these huge increases in liquidity go a long way toward explaining why interest rates did not respond to the surge in public debt. If anything, the real puzzle is not why interest rates did not increase but why inflation remained so low despite the increase in the supply of money. We return to this issue in chapter 7 when we discuss whether printing money could be a permanent solution to the surge in public debt, a question that depends on whether at one point central banks will have to sell on the market the government securities they have purchased over the past seven years. For the moment, it suffices to know that the potentially negative effects of a high and rising public debt on the economy have been muted by the central banks' large purchases of government paper. But what are those negative effects? What are the channels through which high public debt might impair the working of a market economy? This is what we discuss in the next two chapters.

THREE

How High Public Debt Can Cause
a Financial Crisis

I used to think if there was reincarnation, I wanted to come back
as the president or the pope or a .400 baseball hitter. But now I
want to come back as the bond market. You can intimidate
everybody.

—*James Carville*

The first reason why too much public debt is bad for an economy is
that it can lead to a crisis in the government bond market. These crises can be violent, devastating for an economy, and can develop quickly
out of an apparently blue sky. A short story illustrates my point.

On a sunny afternoon in March 2009, while the world was undergoing
the deepest economic crisis since the 1930s, I asked for a confidential
meeting with the managing director of the International Monetary Fund
(IMF), Dominique Strauss-Kahn, whose name would become familiar to
the general public a couple of years later for reasons unrelated to his official responsibilities. I was at that time head of the IMF's Fiscal Affairs Department, and I had asked for a meeting to explain to him the effect that
the economic crisis was having on the fiscal accounts of the world, particularly those of advanced economies. I was not bringing good news.

The economic crisis was causing a surge in public debt as governments
were using public money to support the economy while their tax revenues
were declining as a result of the 2008–09 recession. After describing to

Strauss-Kahn the state of the world's fiscal accounts, I concluded: "Managing Director, the current economic crisis has been caused by banks. The next one will be caused by the government accounts."

"Why?" he asked me, which left me a bit surprised, as I had just given him rather dire forecasts of trends in public debt in the world's economies. I explained that the biggest increase in public debt ever registered in peacetime could raise doubts about governments' ability or willingness to repay their debt, which could lead to a crisis in the government securities market in one or more countries, including some pretty sizable ones.

He did not seem impressed. At that time, government paper markets were relatively quiet: yields on government securities were then still quite low. Only a few months later, problems started showing up, sometimes quite dramatically, in several high-debt countries: Iceland first, followed, in a sort of chain reaction, by Hungary, Greece, Ireland, Portugal, Italy, and Spain.

I mention this story to underscore the point that crises of confidence in government paper markets can develop quite unexpectedly. Suddenly, investors start having doubts about the willingness of the government to repay its debt, and stop buying government paper. The government loses market access (that's how economists and financial market experts describe the situation). When that happens, the whole economy is likely to crash. The inability of the government to borrow, or its ability to borrow only at interest rates that are not sustainable over time, forces the government to cut spending or to raise taxes quickly, which hits the economy immediately. Moreover, borrowing conditions deteriorate for the private sector as well. One might think that if investing in government paper in country A becomes too risky, investors can choose to invest their money in private sector securities in the same country, but that is not so. Investors simply take their investments out of the country, and for good reason. If the government cannot be trusted, why should the private sector be trusted? Perhaps more substantively, if a major fiscal contraction is approaching and the government cannot support the private sector in case of need, why should investors lend to the private sector? When money runs away from a country, however, the economy collapses, GDP declines, and unemployment rises. That is what happened, for example, in Italy in 2011–12: GDP declined in Italy by 4 percent between 2011 and 2013, and the loss was larger compared with what GDP would have been had Italy continued to grow at its potential rate. In Greece, another country where the government lost market access, the crisis was much deeper (see chapter 11). The same scenario unfolded in several emerging economies over the past few decades. It is not a pretty picture, and it often ends in a request for financial support from the IMF and, equally often, in a government crisis.

This chapter looks more closely at the risk of a crisis in the government paper market. When do investors lose confidence in the government's ability or willingness to repay its debt? Why are certain countries at greater risk than others? Which indicators should be used to assess the risk of a crisis? Not all these questions can be answered easily. That is why crises in the government paper market often happen rapidly and unexpectedly. That is also why they are so dangerous, and why countries should not feel safe just because things look good at the moment. Overconfidence can be very costly when it comes to public debt.

Public Debt and Financial Crises: Mr. Ponzi's Lesson

As discussed in chapter 1, every month the government needs to go back to the financial markets to fill the gap between its spending and its revenues (its deficit) and to roll over its maturing securities. Investors are willing to buy the newly issued bonds if they believe they will be repaid when the bonds mature. If they perceive there is a risk they will not be repaid, they will initially require higher interest rates on the bonds to compensate them for the risk of not getting their money back (the *default risk premium*). But as a higher interest rate also makes it more difficult for the borrower to pay back its debt, at some point higher interest rates will no longer provide a sufficient incentive for investors to buy government paper, and they will just stop doing so. The basic question we address in this chapter is this: What leads investors to believe they might not be paid back if they buy government paper?

The main factor is the fear that the government will not have enough resources, in particular resources that have not been borrowed, to service its debt. These resources are given by the government *primary surplus*, that is, by the government revenues minus the government noninterest (or *primary*) *expenditures* (see chapter 1). In other words, the primary surplus must be sufficiently large.

If the primary surplus is not large enough or, worse, if instead of a primary surplus the government is running a primary deficit, then the government borrows not only to pay the interest that is coming due and not only to roll over the securities that are maturing but also to finance an underlying imbalance between revenues and noninterest spending, an imbalance that would exist even in the absence of debt. Then a snowball effect arises: the government borrows faster and faster simply to survive. This can go on for a while until investors understand that the indebted government does not have a flow of primary resources to service its debt. When they realize it does not, and that it has no prospects for having one, everything suddenly collapses. Sooner or later all schemes of this sort—involving a continuous rise in debt at an accelerating pace, fueled by a primary deficit—collapse. They are called Ponzi schemes, after Charles Ponzi, the quintessential villain of American financial history. Let's briefly consider his story as it helps us understand both the similarities and the differences with respect to the issue of public debt sustainability.

Charles Ponzi, born Carlo Ponzi in Lugo di Romagna, Italy, in 1882, emigrated to North America in 1903. After serving time in Canada for cashing a forged check, he moved to Boston, where in early 1920 he set up what later became universally known as a Ponzi scheme. It was certainly not the first of its kind, as Ponzi himself was inspired by the actions of a small Canadian bank, the Zarossi Bank, where he had worked. The scheme involved borrowing money from small savers at a very high rate: Ponzi promised a 50 percent interest rate for a six-month maturity, pretending that the money would be invested in a high-yield arbitrage activity that would generate a sufficiently large "primary surplus." The arbitrage activity involved purchasing international mail coupons (that is, coupons that could be used for mailing letters internationally) in countries such as Italy that had devalued their currency after the war. Those coupons could be exchanged for regular stamps at a rate that had not been adjusted for the postwar depreciation of the currency and thus reflected the prewar exchange rate. This allowed the buyer of the coupons to make a safe profit. However, the number of coupons available was far below what would have been necessary to produce the high profits and pay the huge interest rate promised by Ponzi on his large-scale borrowing.[1] Ponzi's arbitrage activity thus was flawed and did not produce any significant income stream. He was able to repay those investors who wanted their many back at maturity only by borrowing more and more. Of course, the money borrowed by Ponzi was also used to finance his luxurious lifestyle (his "primary deficit").

Ponzi's scheme lasted until he managed to attract new investors to reimburse those (initially) few who decided to leave. But when rumors started spreading that Ponzi had no underlying source of income, the scheme collapsed. At the end of July 1920 the *Boston Post* started publishing articles asking questions that Ponzi could not answer. The collapse was fast, as the number of investors who refused to roll over their credit skyrocketed instantly. Ponzi's assets were not sufficient to face their claims, and on August 13 he was arrested. After spending a few years in jail in the United States, Ponzi returned to Italy, then moved to Brazil (where he worked for a time for Ala Littoria, Italy's airline company during the fascist era), and died in Rio de Janeiro in 1949 a poor man. But his legend lives on, and the term "Ponzi scheme" has an entrenched place in the economic and financial literature.

Ponzi's story tells us two things. First, Ponzi schemes can attract large amounts of money: Ponzi managed to borrow up to $1 million a day, equivalent to some $12 million in today's dollars. Similar schemes in more recent times, like the one set up by Bernie Madoff, who went bust and was arrested in 2008, reached even more amazing heights: the total loss of Madoff's scheme is estimated at about $15 billion. The second lesson to be drawn from Ponzi's story is that these schemes can collapse very quickly. Like many things in financial markets, they are based on confidence, and confidence can be lost amazingly quickly, essentially because the loss of confidence is contagious. Thus one should not take comfort in the fact that the financial weather looks good today. Storms can gather very quickly.

The Advantage Governments Have over Ponzi

What causes a crisis of confidence in the government paper market? To avoid the risk of a confidence crisis, it is critical that investors be convinced that the government is not running a Ponzi scheme and that its primary surplus stream is sufficiently large to ensure the timely payment of the interest that falls due and, potentially, of the securities that will not be rolled over.

The government, however, seemingly has a big advantage with respect to Mr. Ponzi. His scheme could continue only because investors did not have enough information about his underlying activity or know that he was running large primary deficits. They thought the liquidity expressed in his lavish lifestyle came from a profitable activity and not from new borrowing. If they had known that Ponzi had a primary deficit, they would not have lent him a penny. In the case of sovereign states, things are a bit different. Sovereign states can sustain sizable primary deficits over time without major consequences for their ability to borrow, even if published information is available about the underlying imbalance of their accounts, and specifically that their primary surpluses are too small or even negative.

Let's take an example. Suppose a government has revenues amounting to €700 billion, noninterest spending amounting to €720 billion, and interest spending of €70 billion. This government would be running a Ponzi scheme if its revenues and spending did not change over time. Its total deficit would be €90 billion, and it would have to borrow from financial markets not only to roll over maturing securities and not only to pay interest on its outstanding debt but also to finance a primary deficit of €20 billion (€720 billion of noninterest spending minus €700 million of revenues). This could not go on forever. Yet many governments are in exactly this situation: they borrow to finance not only interest payments and maturing debt but also a primary deficit. (By the way, the numbers just given are approximately those of the Italian government in 2009. Italy was running a primary deficit because its fiscal accounts had been hit by the global economic and financial crisis, and tax revenues had declined sharply. But its government paper market did not get into trouble until more than two years later, and no crisis occurred for many governments that are still running primary deficits and, thus, technically running Ponzi schemes.) Of course, governments would deny this: at a closed-door event involving G-20 countries held in 2010, I argued that the governments of many advanced economies, with unchanged policies, were at the time running what could be regarded as Ponzi schemes. The officials who were present at the event, especially a U.S. Treasury high official, were not pleased.

Why do financial markets lend to a government that is seemingly running a Ponzi scheme, even if information is fully available on its revenues and spending? The reason is that, contrary to what happens in a classic Ponzi scheme, the government can change its future revenues and spending and thus improve its primary balance. Markets are willing to lend because they believe the fiscal imbalance is temporary and the government accounts will improve in the future.

How, then, can one decide how risky it is to lend to a government? In theory, it is just a matter of assessing whether the government will be able to raise its primary surplus—by raising taxes or cutting primary spending—to a level that is sufficiently high to service its initial debt, and whether it will be able to maintain over time the required primary balance. How large should the primary balance be? It depends on the debt level: the greater the debt level, the higher is the amount of interest payments that will be required and the larger is the required primary surplus. But raising and maintaining over time a large primary surplus is not easy: it means people must be taxed more or public services must be cut, which in the short run is not good for the economy or for elections. That is the reason why the larger the public debt, the more investors may fear that the government might decide not to pay them back. Thus, the larger the public debt—with respect to GDP, which is the country's income and the base the government can potentially tax to raise its primary surplus—the higher is the risk of a confidence crisis in the government paper market.

Of course, things are more complicated than this. The primary surplus that is needed to avoid the risk of a crisis does not depend on the level of public debt alone but on other factors as well. Two are particularly important. The first one is the growth rate of the economy (the growth rate of GDP); the second is the average interest rate on public debt (which in turn is affected by many factors, some of which were mentioned in chapter 1). Let's look more closely at why the growth rate of the economy and the average interest rate matter, and how.

How the GDP Growth Rate and the Interest Rate on Public Debt Affect Debt Sustainability

Let's start with the GDP growth rate. If the economy is growing rapidly, the primary surplus needed to stabilize the ratio of public debt to GDP is smaller because the weight of debt as a percentage of GDP is eroded by the faster growth of GDP. In other words, growth in GDP can do the same job as the primary surplus in containing the public debt-to-GDP ratio. There is another reason why faster growth can help: in an environment of faster growth, it may be easier to maintain a higher surplus. I defer further discussion of the role of growth in containing the debt-to-GDP ratio to chapter 14.[2]

Let's now move to the average interest rate on public debt: the higher the interest rate the government has to pay, the higher will be its interest payments, for any given amount of debt. Not all debt is the same: some debt is heavy because it bears a higher interest rate, while some is lighter because it bears a lower interest rate. The primary surplus needed to service "lighter" debt is lower because interest payments will be lower (an issue that is discussed with specific reference to the case of Greek public debt in chapter 11). Thus, countries that, for structural reasons and not just temporarily, can borrow at lower interest rates can sustain over time a higher public debt ratio.

Of course, the interest rate paid on public debt depends on the level of debt itself because, as discussed earlier, the higher the public debt, the higher is the risk that an investor will not be paid back and the higher is the risk premium that the investor will demand. However, the interest rate the government has to pay does not depend on the debt level alone but also on other things, some of which were mentioned in chapters 1 and 2. Let me just recap them here and add a few more remarks:

- It makes a big difference whether debt is held by domestic or foreign investors. The latter may be more willing to run away if there are problems, and the temptation to default on public debt is higher if debt is held by foreigners. Thus the default risk premium and the interest rate on public debt may be higher when debt is held externally.

- The average maturity of public debt also matters. Shorter maturities imply higher gross financing needs and also imply that the government needs to test the market confidence more frequently, which also is risky and may raise the risk premium.

- The amount of private debt existing in a country is relevant, at least according to some economists. If the private sector is highly indebted, the risk that it will have to ask for the support of the government at some point in the future is higher, which creates a contingent liability for the government. The quality of the private sector debt also matters, as this affects the likelihood that the private sector will need to receive financial support from the government. This issue has become very topical in recent years with respect to the possibility that governments may be asked to bail out banks. A weak banking system definitely creates sizable risks for the government and may have an impact on the risk premium.

- The amount of public debt held by the central bank, and more generally the monetary policy stance, are very important in affecting the interest rate on public debt. Here, however, the key question is how long central banks will be able to absorb government securities without causing too much inflation (see chapter 7).

▪ Finally, the dynamics of the public debt ratio matter. Econometric work that I have undertaken with some IMF colleagues, Antonio Bassanetti and Andrea Presbitero, shows that what causes a rollover crisis is not high debt but high and rising debt. This makes sense: if markets see that debt is rising from an already high level, they will get nervous because the primary surplus needed to stabilize the debt or bring it down will become more and more demanding. Our results also show that if the public debt-to-GDP ratio is declining by, say, five percentage points of GDP per year, the probability of a crisis falls by more than 35 percent with respect to a case in which the debt ratio is constant, and even more with respect to the case of rising debt. This is good news for many countries with high debt: they will start benefiting from a process of debt reduction even if the debt ratio remains high (see chapter 15).

Shortcuts to Assess When Public Debt Involves Excessive Risks

Thus many factors affect the level of risk associated with a certain public debt-to-GDP level, which explains why some countries, such as the United States, seem able to sustain a high public debt level without getting into much trouble. That said, it may still be useful to look at the public debt-to-GDP ratio, at least as a starting point for further analysis: though high debt may not be a sufficient condition for getting into trouble, it is likely to be a necessary condition. In this respect, several studies have tried to identify "debt thresholds" beyond which the risk of getting into trouble may rise more significantly, thresholds that can be used as shortcuts to assess the degree of exposure to crisis risks. While different thresholds are available, I present those currently used by the IMF, which over the past few years has stepped up its work on public debt sustainability.

The IMF uses different thresholds for advanced and emerging economies. Financial markets in the latter are less developed, which makes it more difficult for their governments to borrow from domestic markets at relatively contained interest rates and moves them toward riskier external borrowing.

The threshold used for emerging markets is currently 70 percent: beyond that level the IMF undertakes a more in-depth analysis of the other features of public debt that may increase or reduce the risk of a rollover crisis. The threshold for advanced economies is somewhat higher, 85 percent. Several advanced economies—including all the major ones except Germany—currently have debt ratios that exceed this threshold.

These figures have to be taken with a grain of salt, particularly those for advanced economies. Because the risk of a crisis is affected by several factors in addition to the level of public debt, debt thresholds are only partial indicators. Moreover, those thresholds come from statistical analyses that look at the past and evaluate at what level of debt ratios countries got into trouble. But this is particularly tricky for advanced economies because there have been few cases of turmoil in government paper markets over the past decades for advanced economies until the wave of crises in the euro zone in 2011–12. So we do not know much about the actual degree of risk exposure to government debt crises in advanced economies. Will debt crises in advanced economies become a regular feature of the future, or were the 2011–12 episodes one-off events, perhaps related to the idiosyncrasies of the euro zone? We are sailing in uncharted waters because public debt in advanced economies has never been so high except as a result of wars and in periods when financial markets were much more constrained than they are now. All this calls for some caution. In any case, public debt ratios well in excess of 85 percent are certainly not good news for advanced economies.

Why Should We Worry If Interest Rates Are So Low?

The low interest rates on government paper that currently prevail in almost all advanced economies (Greece is an exception) suggest we should not worry too much about the high level of public debt. After all, did we not just say that the sustainability of public debt depends on the average interest rate on debt? There is definitely some truth to this, at least in the short run, but one's thinking should not be overly influenced by the current situation. Indeed, the problem is that the currently low interest rates can lead to a false sense of security.

Let me stress once more that by their very nature, financial market conditions can change very rapidly. For example, the 2011–12 sovereign debt crisis in the euro zone was preceded by years of low interest rates on all government securities in the euro zone. Even as late as the spring of 2011 the spread between the yield of Italian and German government bonds was about 160 basis points (below the current level, although higher than it had been before the 2008–09 crisis), but by the end of the year it had risen to some 550 basis points, an unsustainable level. These sudden changes often reflect the way financial markets work, and more specifically what economists call "feedback loops," processes that reinforce each other and spiral out of control. Economists also sometimes talk of "multiple equilibria" to describe situations in which, triggered by some event, markets move quickly from one position to another without an underlying change in fundamentals. How can this happen in government paper markets? Suppose some investors start having doubts about the ability of one government to service its debt. This will lead to higher interest rates on government securities. If public debt is low, this does not affect very much the fiscal accounts. But when public debt is high, the impact on the fiscal accounts is stronger. This stronger impact will make other investors believe that the public debt is not sustainable, and this belief in turn will lead to a further rise in interest rates. A chain reaction may take hold as more and more investors start believing that the debt is unsustainable. But as interest rates rise, public debt does become unsustainable, through a process of self-fulfilling expectations, because the primary surplus needed to service it becomes larger and larger. Investors may also become worried that the spending cuts and tax increases needed to raise the primary surplus will hurt the economy and depress growth. If GDP does decline, investors start worrying even more, which also pushes interest rates up. And this process may happen quite quickly. That is what happened in Italy in 2011–12: a sudden crisis led markets to believe that Italy would not be able to stay in the euro zone, which added another dimension to risk—the possibility of being repaid not in euros but in "new lire."

Finally, very dangerous feedback loops can arise from the interaction of the balance sheet of the government and the balance sheet of banks when the latter have invested heavily in government securities. A rise in the interest rate on government paper lowers the value of the government bonds already in the bank's portfolios, which makes the bank even worse off. If banks are in trouble, this is likely to further drive up the risk premium on government paper because of the potential need for the government to intervene in support of banks, and the process repeats itself. It is a very dangerous spiral from which Italy, Spain, and Portugal have suffered in the past.

So, even if interest rates are low now, one should remain concerned about the potential effects of high public debt on financial stability. Interest rates will not stay low forever, and they have already started rising in some countries, including the United States, where inflation has edged up. At one point, all the money that central banks created since 2008 will have to be mopped up, and that is when the weight of government debt will become more apparent. So we should remain worried. How worried depends, however, on a number of factors that differ across countries. It is time to name names. To what extent are the main countries exposed to the risk of a loss of confidence in their fiscal solvency?

Naming Names

Germany's public debt ratio, after rising to more than 80 percent of GDP in 2010, has now fallen below 70 percent of GDP and is projected to continue to decline, reflecting Germany's primary surplus, its balanced budget (Germany's deficit is close to zero), and its relatively high GDP growth. Moreover, part of Germany's debt is held by the European Central Bank (ECB), thanks to the latter's programs of large purchases of government securities discussed above, which adds stability to its investor base. Germany's only weakness is represented by a relatively high pension debt (see figure 2-4), but the financial markets do not seem to give much weight to pension debt, at least when regular financial debt is relatively low. One should not be surprised, then, if German government securities are regarded as the quintessential safe assets. When there are problems in financial markets and risk appetite declines, the demand for *Bund* (the German word for bonds) surges and their yield declines even more. All this means we should look elsewhere to find areas of risk.

The government securities of two other major countries benefit from being regarded as "safe assets" whose yields usually decline when there is a "flight to safety": those of the United States and Japan. It is far less obvious than in the case of Germany why these countries should be regarded as risk-free, particularly in a medium-term perspective.

Public debt in the United States exceeds 100 percent of GDP. This figure, not the 75 percent often reported in the media, is the real amount of public debt if we include not only the federal government debt but also state and local government debt (see chapter 2). Public debt as a share of

GDP has been rising every year since 2007 because of large deficits. The deficit, after surging to more than 10 percent of GDP in 2009–10, later declined, though it is still fairly high (close to 4.5 percent of GDP in 2016), the second largest deficit (after Spain's) among all thirty-five countries classified as advanced by the IMF. And the U.S. government still runs a sizable primary deficit (over 2 percent of GDP). This is why, despite fairly good growth and relatively low interest rates, the U.S. public debt-to-GDP ratio is still rising, though marginally by now. The United States also faces large pension and health care debt, owing to an aging population and a welfare system in need of further reforms. So why are U.S. government securities regarded as safe assets? Well, first, the above debt figure overestimates somewhat the debt problem. As noted in chapter 2, a sizable chunk of U.S. debt is held by the Federal Reserve (the Fed) and by foreign central banks, which are likely to continue to hold that debt as long as the dollar continues to be regarded as a reserve currency. So the possibility of a default of the United States is quite remote at present, although in 2011 Standard and Poor's downgraded the rating of U.S. government bonds from AAA to AA+. Indeed, many would regard a crisis of confidence in the U.S. government paper market as inconceivable. Yes, from time to time, there is talk of a possible technical default should the U.S. Congress not lift, in a timely way, the legal ceiling on the issuance of government paper. Lifting the ceiling is necessary as long as U.S. public debt continues to increase in dollar terms. So far, however, Congress has always stopped short of causing such a severe disturbance on international financial markets. In any case, that would be a technical and self-inflicted default, not one caused by a confidence crisis. And yet over the longer term there are some risks. The status of reserve currency is not written in stone, and confidence may eventually weaken if public debt keeps rising as a result of rising pressure on welfare spending. Those who believe that a flight from the U.S. government paper market is impossible have sometimes asked me, "Where else would the money go?" I am pretty sure investors would find a place to park their money if they were concerned about rollover problems. The Fed has now started raising interest rates and at some point will probably have to offload in the market the large holdings of U.S. government securities in its portfolio as part of the process of tightening monetary conditions to contain inflation. Finally, the United States has so far been unable to define a medium-term plan to address its still fairly large primary and overall deficit. Bottom line: I would not be worried for a while, but over the longer term some adjustment will be needed. And yet the new Trump administration does not seem to be much concerned and is reportedly planning a stimulus package involving tax cuts and increases in infrastructure spending. The hope is to lower public debt by raising GDP growth through a fiscal expansion. Chapter 14 discusses why this is unlikely to succeed.

Some adjustment will definitely be needed in Japan too to avoid the risk of troubles that now seem remote. The deficit (more than 10 percent of GDP in 2009) has gradually declined but was still over 4 percent of GDP in 2016, one of the largest among the advanced economies. As a result, government gross debt reached 250 percent of GDP in 2016, or 130 percent net of the large holdings of financial assets by the government, fifty percentage points above the 2007 level. However, virtually all of the increase in public debt has been purchased by the Bank of Japan. This has added further resilience, in the immediate future, to the traditional reason why Japan seems to have been shielded from pressure on its government paper market despite its large debt, namely, the strong share of debt held by Japanese residents, more than 90 percent. Thus, currently not only is Japan's public debt held primarily by Japanese investors but a large share of it is now held by Japan's central bank. The huge impact of the massive purchases of government paper by the Bank of Japan is also underscored by the fact that in 2016, the ratio of the government's interest payments to GDP was, amazingly, close to zero (0.2 percent of GDP). Indeed, Japan's deficit almost entirely consists of its primary component (the primary deficit in 2016 was 4 percent of GDP, the largest by far among the advanced economies). Does all this mean Japan is not running risks? Not really. All will work well as long as Japanese investors decide not to diversify their securities portfolio and as long as banks continue to hold huge amounts of deposits at the Bank of Japan (the electronic money held by banks at home created by purchases of government securities by the central bank) rather than, say, using that money to invest abroad. Should investments move, there would likely be financial stability problems in Japan, as interest rates would have to start rising to avoid an excessively rapid offloading of yen-denominated assets. A rise in interest rates would be quite dangerous for banks because of the capital loss they would suffer if the price of bonds declined: it has been computed that a one percentage point increase in interest rates would reduce the capital of Japanese banks by one-fourth. That is why fiscal adjustment is also needed in Japan even if Japan currently is not facing any difficulty in rolling over its debt.

The United Kingdom is in a similar position as Japan but not as extreme. Its deficit is fairly sizable (more than 3 percent of GDP in 2016, with a primary component of 1.5 percent of GDP) but much smaller than Japan's. The same is true of the public debt: high but not as high as Japan's (close to 90 percent of GDP). And a large chunk of it is held by the bank of England (some twenty percentage points of GDP), thanks to large purchases of government bonds by printing electronic money since 2008. Again, there seems to be no immediate risk as long as U.K. banks are happy to hold unprecedentedly large amounts of the idle deposits at the Bank of England. How long will it last?

So far, apart from Germany, we have considered countries where large purchases of government paper by the central bank have muted the impact of the surge in government debt on government interest rates and the risk of a crisis. Granted, there are risks for these countries as well, and we return to this issue in chapter 7, which discusses examples of countries that came under pressure precisely because their central banks were financing the government too much. However, these risks are perhaps of less immediate concern. The advanced-economy countries that got into serious trouble in 2011–12—Greece, Portugal, Ireland, Spain, Italy, and Cyprus—were all in the euro zone and so did not have their own central bank that could buy government paper at will. In all those countries the public debt is still large (well above 100 percent of GDP in Italy, Portugal, and Greece) and is to different degrees still more subject to market pressures: whenever markets get nervous, their yield spreads over the German bund rise rapidly. Greece is a case on its own, as now most of its government debt is no longer held by the private sector but by euro-zone institutions and governments. Ireland is benefiting from strong growth and is in the process of reducing its public debt ratio rapidly, while Spain's debt is still essentially stable at close to 100 percent of GDP despite strong growth because of the still large primary deficit. In Italy and Portugal the process of debt reduction is impeded by a very low growth rate. Financial market pressures in all these countries have abated considerably since 2011, thanks not only to improvements in their primary balances but also to the increasingly large purchases of government paper by the ECB.

This has led some to believe that these countries are off the hook, and public opinion in many of them has turned very critical of the austerity policies that were implemented after 2010 to correct their fiscal imbalances. If interest rates are so low, why should they continue a painful fiscal adjustment? Regrettably, one cannot hope interest rates will remain so low forever in the euro zone, and as long as these countries continue to have high debt, they remain particularly exposed to shocks that may hit the world economy and interest rates. The ECB will continue to keep interest rates low for a while, but that state of affairs will not last forever. Once the European economy and inflation start recovering faster, interest rates will rise. Probably the difference between inflation and interest rates, which is what matters for the dynamics of the public debt ratio, will also rise, as this is what normally happens when interest rates rise. Moreover, something that is often forgotten is that the supportive action of the ECB through its large purchases of government paper, while motivated by the goal of moving inflation from the currently low levels to the ECB objective of "close but below 2 percent," is partly conditional on the continuation of fiscal adjustment over time. Or, in more explicit terms, the continuation of a process of fiscal adjustment in the euro zone may be the necessary condition for Germany and other northern European countries not to raise too many objections to the expansionary monetary policies of the ECB. In any case, Mario Draghi's term as president of the ECB expires in 2019, and his successor may come from one of the very northern European countries that feel less at ease with relaxed monetary conditions. All this suggests that in Europe as well, low interest rates will not last forever, and that pressures on the fiscal accounts of high-debt countries will rise in the not too distant future.

FOUR

How High Public Debt Can Reduce Economic Growth

It must, indeed, be one of these two events; either the nation must destroy public credit, or public credit will destroy the nation.

—*David Hume*

Most economists probably believe that the risk of a financial crisis in the government paper market is a concrete one for many high-debt countries. They believe it because they have seen it happen over recent decades in several emerging economies and, more recently, in some advanced economies as well. Granted, the possibility of a government paper market crisis in the United States seems remote at present, but if there is no correction to current welfare spending trends, problems will likely arise even for the United States in the long run.

High public debt can harm economic growth even in the absence of a financial crisis, however, and it does so in a less apparent and less spectacular, yet no less dangerous way. Two channels are particularly relevant. The first is pretty simple: high public debt reduces the space the government has to support the economy through increases in spending and tax cuts in case of a recession. This is something most economists would agree on, and in a way it is a by-product of the crisis risks discussed in the previous chapter: if public debt is already high, you do not have much fiscal space to maneuver in case a recession hits you. The second channel is more controversial and not all economists would agree it is relevant, at least in advanced economies: high public debt reduces the long-term growth potential of an economy.

To clarify how these two channels operate, it is essential to focus on some concepts that economists often use to explain what causes GDP growth, and in particular how fiscal policy can affect it, for better or worse. The material presented in this chapter is key to understanding not only the advantages arising from maintaining a lower public debt but also the costs that have to be faced in the process of transitioning from a higher to a lower debt level. So it is worthwhile reading this chapter carefully, particularly for noneconomists.

GDP, Potential GDP, and Fiscal Policy

Let's imagine the whole economy is made up of a single car factory. How many cars will this factory produce? Suppose the factory can produce, without overheating its machinery or asking its workers to do more than normal overtime, 1,000 cars a year. That is its normal production capacity. The factory, however, will actually produce 1,000 cars only if its management believes it can sell 1,000 cars, and if there is no need for restocking or for reducing inventories. Thus, in the short run (which means without increasing production capacity), the number of cars produced will depend on the demand for cars.

Now let's move from one factory to the whole economy. What determines output (GDP) in the short run is the demand for all goods and services (economists call this *aggregate demand*), as long as it is not too distant from the production capacity of the whole economy, that is, from its potential output or potential GDP. This is one key element of the theory of income determination developed by John Maynard Keynes in the 1930s in his *General Theory of Employment, Income and Money*. He called his theory "general" because it also worked when the economy was not operating at full capacity.

In the short run, then, output depends on demand. However, when the car factory reaches its potential production of 1,000 cars, a further increase in demand will not cause a further sizable increase in production: for a while the car factory management could raise production above potential but at the cost of overheating its plants or its workers. To avoid this, the factory would rather respond to a rise in demand simply by raising prices, unless it decides to increase its potential output by buying new machinery and hiring more workers. The same holds for the economy as a whole: in the long run (that is, when the economy operates at full capacity), GDP depends on its potential level, and its growth will be determined by how much potential output can grow through new investments and increases in the labor force.

How Is GDP Affected by Fiscal Deficits and Public Debt in the Short Run?

Having clarified these concepts, let's now ask: How is GDP affected by fiscal policy? Let's consider first the short run, that is, a situation in which GDP is determined by the demand side—for cars in our example, or by aggregate demand for the whole economy. A reduction in the fiscal deficit through an increase in taxation or a reduction in public spending will, other conditions being the same, cause a reduction in aggregate demand because people will have less money in their pockets. Thus, in the short run, cutting the fiscal deficit will usually lead to a lower GDP level. Conversely, an increase in the fiscal deficit has an expansionary effect on GDP unless the economy is already operating at full capacity—the 1,000 cars in our example—in which case the only thing that can rise is the car price.[1] This is the main reason why fiscal austerity undertaken to reduce public debt is regarded as bad for the economy and, some argue, should be avoided by anyone who is not a masochist.

Indeed, it cannot be denied—even if some economists do deny it, and rightly so in some circumstances—that in the short run, fiscal tightening is likely to slow aggregate demand and GDP growth. This does not mean that fiscal tightening is always wrong: it may be necessary, for example, when the economy is overheating and is producing at above capacity. It may also be needed when it is necessary to avoid worse outcomes, such as when the fiscal accounts are on an unsustainable path and there is a risk of a financial crisis. But the short-term negative impact of fiscal tightening needs to be taken into account at least in deciding the pace of fiscal adjustment.

So far we have discussed the short-term impact of changes in the fiscal deficit on economic activity. How about the impact of high debt? High public debt can affect growth even in the short run because high debt makes it more difficult for the government to increase the fiscal deficit because a higher deficit will raise public debt even more, which could cause the kind of confidence crisis described in the previous chapter. In other words, running Keynesian aggregate demand policies will be more difficult when public debt is high. It is not clear how much Keynes himself regarded the accumulation of public debt as a major impediment to the implementation of Keynesian policies. Keynes never wrote anything on this issue. However, according to Abba Lerner, during a meeting in Washington in 1943 at which the risk of a prolonged shortfall in aggregate demand in the aftermath of World War II was discussed among a group of prominent economists, in response to Lerner's view that the lack of aggregate demand could be offset for a long time by public spending financed by higher public debt, Keynes answered in the following way (as reported by Lerner): "He said, you mean the national debt will keep on growing, and I said yes, 'what would happen?' I said—nothing. So we talked for a moment and he said: 'No, that's humbug'—that's the word he used, humbug—'the national debt can't keep on growing.'"[2]

In any case, the hypothesis that high public debt constrains the possibility of using fiscal policy to support the economy is broadly shared by economists. This constraint has been experienced, for example, by Italy in 2008 and 2009, when the support the Italian government could give to the economy had to be much smaller than what was being provided by other governments that had accumulated less debt in the past. Thus, an additional rationale for reducing public debt is to create fiscal space that would allow fiscal policy to be used to boost economic activity if necessary when the economy is weak.

Public Debt and Potential Output

The level of public debt can also affect potential output. This is a much less visible effect, certainly much less visible than a full-blown financial crisis. The country, rather than suffering from a stroke, withers slowly. Somewhat colorfully, the media like to talk about growth being dragged down by the burden of public debt. I believe that it is a real risk, but it is important to clarify how high public debt can reduce potential growth, not least because not all economists believe it is a major issue worth talking about in practice.

Let's go back to the example of the car factory. As we discussed, in the long run the number of cars that is produced depends on the factory's production capacity. And production capacity depends on how many people are employed by the factory and on the availability of machinery, and hence on management's investment decisions. Now, there are two ways to explain why high public debt can lower the potential capacity of our factory, and of potential GDP for the whole economy. The first one is that, to avoid a confidence crisis, high public debt requires running a larger primary surplus, which requires higher taxes, and this will discourage investment. Higher taxes will also discourage labor supply and hence the possibility for the car factory to increase employment. This is an idea as old as economics. David Ricardo, one of the fathers of economics, was already talking about it in 1817 in his *Principles of Economic Policy and Taxation*: an entrepreneur will prefer to invest abroad if the taxes needed to service public debt are too high.[3] This argument can also be used in a forward-looking way: debt will have to be repaid sooner or later, and repaying debt will mean tax increases. Finally, a variant of this argument—quite often used in the United States by both media and analysts—is that high interest payments on public debt will bring about not higher taxes but cuts in pro-growth government spending, such as public investment, education, or important safety net programs. In the words of Erskine Bowles, a cochair of President Barack Obama's bipartisan deficit-reduction commission, the National Commission on Fiscal Responsibility and Reform, known more simply as the Simpson-Bowles commission: "We'll be spending over $1 trillion a year on interest by 2020. That's $1 trillion we can't spend to educate our kids or to replace our badly worn-out infrastructure."[4]

The second way to explain how high public debt can drag down growth looks at the effect of public debt on interest rates: high public debt will make it more difficult for our car factory to borrow to finance new investment because the available private saving will be absorbed by the public sector; interest rates, other conditions being the same, will be higher, and this will discourage new private investment. This is the mechanism economists refer to as "crowding out": too much public debt crowds out private debt from savers' portfolios. Various theoretical models are available to explain in more detail this process.[5] In the words of Alan Greenspan, chairman of the Federal Reserve from August 1987 to January 2006:

> I have long argued that paying down the national debt is beneficial for the economy: it keeps interest rates lower than they otherwise would be and frees savings to finance increases in the capital stock, thereby boosting productivity and real incomes.[6]

Arguing that high public debt harms the potential growth of an economy is, of course, a statement with deep political connotations. High public debt is bad because it involves higher taxes and crowds out private debt. Private debt is good, public debt is bad. Taxes and public spending are bad, private investment is good. It does not sound too scientific, right? After all, one could also argue that if public spending and debt are used to finance good infrastructure and good public education, they can also benefit potential growth. So who is right and who is wrong?

If we look at the statistical relationship between public debt and long-term growth, we see something quite clear: countries with high public debt are countries that, over the longer term, have shown lower growth. Among all advanced economies, the three countries that over the past twenty-five years have had the lowest growth have been Japan, Italy, and Greece. Over the same period these three countries have also had on average the highest public debt. However, the interpretation of this negative correlation is not straightforward because of the possibility of reverse causality. Some argue that when the economy grows less, government revenues are lower, and governments may not be willing to cut spending (at least for a while), which leads to fiscal deficits and the accumulation of debt. It is not high debt that would cause low growth. It is low growth that would cause high debt.

One of the first studies to argue, after the 2008–09 surge in public debt, that high public debt could harm potential output growth was based on simple statistical evidence that did not consider the possibility of reverse causality. I refer to "Growth in a Time of Debt," by Ken Rogoff of Harvard University and Carmen Reinhart of the Harvard Kennedy School, both well-known economists.[7] Moreover, it turned out that their study included some computational errors. This somewhat discredited the view that high public debt negatively affects potential growth. However, most of the later work done using more appropriate statistical tools found that there is indeed a line of causality moving from high public debt to low growth. According to some of these studies there is a "threshold effect": up to a certain level, more public debt is good for growth, but beyond that level more public debt is harmful, the threshold being 40 to 50 percent of GDP according to some studies, 80 to 90 percent of GDP according to others.[8] By how much is potential growth lowered? A 2010 paper by Manmohan S. Kumar and Jaejoon Woo, economists in the Fiscal Affairs Department of the IMF, concluded that a country with a public debt ratio of 120 percent, other conditions being the same, will have a potential growth rate 1 percent lower than a country with a public debt ratio of 60 percent.[9] This is quite a lot: it is the effect on the annual growth rate, which means that, after twenty years, the income gap between the two countries will have increased by 22 percent.

Some studies have, however, concluded that the level of public debt is not the only thing that matters; also important is whether public debt is rising or declining as a ratio to GDP. A 2014 paper by Andrea Pescatori, Damiano Sandri, and John Simon, economists in the Research Department of the IMF, finds not only that there is indeed a negative relationship between high public debt and growth (although there is no specific threshold) but also that the relationship disappears if the public debt-to-GDP ratio is declining.[10] This is good news for high public debt countries: it takes a long time to lower public debt by using standard fiscal adjustment tools. However, if a high but declining debt-to-GDP ratio is not as harmful as a high but stable debt-to-GDP ratio, countries pursuing debt reduction policies will be able to move onto a faster potential growth path even if, for a while, public debt remains high.

Altogether, there is enough empirical evidence to conclude that countries with high public debt-to-GDP ratios will tend to grow less over the medium term, particularly if the ratio is not declining at a sufficient pace, and this occurs regardless of whether high public debt does or does not lead to a financial crisis.

FIVE

Public Debt, Moral Imperatives, and Politics

The principle of spending money to be paid by posterity, under the name of funding, is but swindling futurity on a large scale.

—Thomas Jefferson

Moral arguments are quite commonly used, often by politicians, to explain why public debt is bad and should be reduced. These arguments often appeal to human instincts rather than to human rationality and sound, objective arguments. But they are not less important as they often work in forging consensus and, after all, I find some of them quite appealing.

Love

The most commonly used moral argument for lowering public debt is that high public debt hurts our children, who will have to repay it. It is not fair to dump on them the results of our prodigality. If we love them, we should not leave them public debt as inheritance. While this argument is tremendously appealing from a media perspective (who doesn't love children?), it only holds fully if public debt is held entirely by foreigners: if foreigners today lend money to the state (and to us, as users of public services), that money tomorrow will have to be repaid tomorrow by the state (that is, by our children, through their taxes). If instead public debt is held entirely by domestic residents, the argument does not hold. If debt is held by residents, some residents today are lending money to the government to finance spending in support of other (or all) residents. When the debt tomorrow will have to be repaid, our children (tomorrow's residents) will be taxed to repay other residents (the children of those who lent money to the government). In other words, you leave public debt as an inheritance to all, but you also leave a credit toward the state to at least some. Some politicians have clearly understood this, including, long ago, Franklin Delano Roosevelt, who, in a speech delivered on May 22, 1939, said: "Our national debt after all is an internal debt owed not only by the Nation but to the Nation. If our children have to pay interest on it they will pay that interest to themselves."[1]

As we have seen, the share of public debt owned domestically varies widely across advanced countries, being as high as 90 percent in Japan but lower than 20 percent in smaller countries such as Austria, Finland, Latvia, and Lithuania. So, for countries with a large share of public debt held domestically, this argument does not really work. That said, to put off making difficult fiscal policy decisions to tomorrow—leaving them to our children—does imply leaving the country exposed to the costs and risks arising from high public debt: it means leaving as an inheritance tough choices and, in the process, jeopardizing the basis for strong future growth.

Sin

Let's move to other moral arguments. A moral distaste for debt characterizes the attitude toward public debt in some northern European countries (Germany, Finland, the Netherlands). The underlying idea is that borrowing is somewhat sinful. The German word for guilt is *Schuld*, and its plural, *Schulden*, means debts or liabilities, a linguistic relationship that, by the way, exists in other European languages, as well as in extinct languages such as Aramaic and Sanskrit.[2]

Returning to the fiscal accounts, to avoid permanent debt accumulation the government budget should balance, at least on average over the years. Borrowing, on the other hand, means a tendency to spend more than what is available; it means believing that it is right to consume more than what you earn, putting off to tomorrow the resolution of today's problems, and being unable to make painful decisions. But as one German proverb says, "Lieber ein Ende mit Schrecken als ein Schrecken ohne Ende," which means, more or less, a painful end is better than an endless pain, or, in other words, procrastinating is wrong.

Free Riding

An additional interpretation of some countries' aversion to increasing public debt and sizable budget deficits is available: weak fiscal balances are seen as the outcome of dumping on the public sector responsibilities and tasks that do not properly belong to it. Asking the government to provide public services that are not financed by taxes is tantamount to dumping on an entity perceived as external (as a collective) the shortcomings of individuals. It is free riding.

Such a vision of public deficits and debt is quite common in the United States and in the United Kingdom, at least since Margaret Thatcher's government.[3] Many conservative American politicians have often used this kind of reasoning to argue against public debt: people need to take care of themselves and not ask the government to take care of them. The words of Cicero, the Roman orator and politician, are often quoted in support of the view that public debt is morally wrong because it implies excessive reliance on public welfare:

> The budget should be balanced, the treasury should be refilled, public debt should be reduced, the arrogance of officialdom should be tempered and controlled, and the assistance to foreign lands should be curtailed lest Rome become bankrupt. People must again learn to work, instead of living on public assistance.

The quote is apocryphal but clarifies well the motivation of some American conservatives to oppose public spending, deficits, and debt.[4]

A More Objective View

These moral arguments against public debt sometimes have a weak objective basis, particularly if taken to their extreme consequences, including especially the need to erase public debt and to balance the budget at all times and in all countries. With regard to the distaste for public deficits on general principles, it should be noted that the definition of deficit used for the government budget is different from the one used for the private sector. This is because government spending includes public investment (to build schools, roads, and so on) and hence includes something that increases the stock of public assets. For a private firm, investment spending is not regarded as a cost and therefore does not affect the bottom line (only the depreciation over time of capital is included as spending). This prudential approach in defining public debt may be justified in the case of the public sector, for example because investment spending, even if it generates an asset, also contributes to the increase in public debt that exposes the public sector balance sheet to rollover risks. But if the government invests in useful public goods, it is not wasting money, and some of the arguments against public debt are weakened. Finally, as discussed in chapters 3 and 4, avoiding the shortcomings arising from excessive public debt does not require eliminating public debt altogether. It simply requires keeping the ratio between public debt and GDP relatively low. Public debt does not need to be repaid fully.

That said, the moral arguments against public debt are not entirely far-fetched. Indeed, high fiscal imbalances are often the result of a culture prone to dumping on the public sector responsibilities and costs that should be borne by private individuals. With regard to Italy, my country, I was impressed by a television debate I watched some time ago that focused on the possibility that the state might take care of the additional costs a couple sustains when the partnership breaks up. The debate was not over whether or not the state should bear those costs (it was somewhat taken for granted that the state should) but over whether the state should bear the costs if the separating couple was not legally married.

It is also worth noting that the moral aversion to public debt and to shifting to the public sector costs that should be borne by individuals is not solely part of the genetic code of the political right. It also belongs to some part of the political left.

Indeed, some prominent right-wing politicians have never been particularly concerned about building up public debt. Ronald Reagan once jokingly said, "I am not worried about the deficit. It is big enough to take care of itself." Not surprisingly, during his two presidencies, U.S. public debt increased from 40 percent to 60 percent of GDP. And in 2004, Dick Cheney confidently stated that "Reagan proved that deficits don't matter." The nonchalance of some right-wing U.S. politicians with regard to public debt is also found in other countries, including Italy, where, with the exception of Marco Minghetti, prime minister and finance minister in the 1870s (and the only one who managed to balance Italy's fiscal budget), the political right has never been particularly concerned about the soundness of the public accounts.

In stark contrast, President John F. Kennedy called for individual responsibility in his inaugural address of January 20, 1961: "Ask not what your country can do for you, ask what you can do for your country."

Turning now to Europe, and particularly to Italy, many still remember the two speeches given in 1977 by Enrico Berlinguer, the Italian Communist Party's charismatic leader, in praise of austerity as a value of the left. He noted in one speech from January 15:

Austerity means rectitude, efficiency, seriousness, and it means social justice; that is the opposite of all we have known and paid for so far and that has caused the current severe crisis whose damages have been building up for years and that we are now experiencing in full in Italy.

And in another speech, given January 30:

A more austere society can also be more just society, less unfair, truly freer, more democratic, more humane.[5]

There is another reason why the political left should dislike public debt. A country cannot be truly free if its destiny is determined by the vagaries of financial markets. An indebted country is subject to speculative attacks. We may dislike speculators, but what makes speculation possible is a country's exposure to it owing to its high debt. As an Italian, I am tired of seeing my country's destiny being decided by foreign investors in London or Frankfurt. If countries like Italy do not lower their public debt, they will always remain slaves of financial markets. That is something the political left should appreciate.

Altogether, enforcing a balance constraint on the state and other public administrations is consistent with the need to fight the free lunch syndrome: people should not get a free lunch simply by asking the government to pay. It is also consistent with the need to avoid the risks and costs arising from high public debt discussed in chapters 3 and 4. These risks and costs should be acknowledged by both the political right and the political left. The two sides of the political spectrum may disagree on what the government should do to meet its budget constraint, but not on the fact that building up too much debt is problematic. If anything, what characterizes the position of those who care for the soundness of the public accounts is not their political coloration but an inclination to take a long view of economic policy decisions—as opposed to policy decisions driven by the electoral cycle—and the recognition that, sooner or later, the fiscal accounts must be sound, or troubles will follow. To sum it up, a budget constraint does not have a political color.

SIX

A Pause to Recap

Once you eliminate the impossible, whatever remains, no matter
how improbable, must be the truth.

—*Sir Arthur Conan Doyle*

This short chapter links the first part of the book, explaining why high
public debt is a problem, with the second and third parts of the book,
which focus on the solutions to the problem. It gives us a chance to recap
and see where we stand.

High public debt is a problem for three reasons. First, it exposes countries to the risks of financial instability. While this instability would arise
initially in the government paper market, it could cause serious damage to
the whole economy. Second, high debt can harm growth even in the absence of a crisis by slowing down potential growth through higher interest
rates or through the higher taxation and lower productive spending needed
to service the debt stock, as well as by preventing the government from using
fiscal policy to respond to economic shocks in the absence of sufficient fiscal
space. Third is the moral argument, perhaps somewhat less concrete yet
quite powerful for many: living with high debt is a symptom of, but could
also foster, negative social attitudes, such as dumping on the collective the
various responsibilities that belong to the individual.

One should not go overboard in demonizing public debt. Yes, in my view the current level of public debt in many advanced countries is too high, but solving the problem does not require paying back the whole amount of public debt. What is necessary is to lower the level of public debt with respect to the size of the economy, that is, with respect to GDP. This means that public debt needs to grow less rapidly than GDP, which would reduce the ratio between the former and the latter. Moreover, how fast the debt ratio should be reduced varies across countries because even countries with the same level of public debt ratios are not equally exposed to risk. Finally, even as a percentage of GDP, the public debt ratio does not need to fall indefinitely. There is no economic reason why it should be zero or even very low. What is a reasonable long-term target for the public debt-to-GDP ratio? Again, this depends on country circumstances, but I would say there is no evidence that a public debt-to-GDP ratio of, say, 40 to 60 percent involves major drawbacks for advanced economies, particularly if, through entitlement reform, a country manages to reduce what we called pension and health care debt. A 40 to 60 percent of GDP level would in any event allow sufficient room for fiscal policy to be used to support economic activity in case of an economic recession without approaching too closely that level of 85 percent of GDP that the International Monetary Fund (IMF) regards as signaling increased risks. And, for countries in the European Union, a public debt level below 60 percent of GDP is also in line with the fiscal rules of that region.

So, it would be nice to have a debt ratio of 40 to 60 percent of GDP. But if you start from a higher level, should public debt really be lowered? Arguing that high public debt involves costs for the economy does not necessarily imply that it should be lowered. The reason is that lowering public debt also involves costs. Readers may have noticed that some of the costs arising from high public debt would also arise during, and may even be magnified by, the process of reducing it. Take, for example, the negative impact on potential growth arising from high debt because the latter forces the government to keep taxes higher or productive public spending lower than would otherwise be necessary. Well, lowering public debt, at least if it is done through what we may call orthodox fiscal adjustment, would involve keeping taxes even higher or spending even lower, though only temporarily, if the goal is to lower the public debt ratio and not just keep it stable at a higher level (this issue is discussed further in chapter 15). Another example: we have seen that, if public debt is high, it will not be possible for the government to use the fiscal lever to support the economy when it is weak. But if, to repay public debt and regain fiscal space, we need to tighten fiscal policy, are we not weakening the economy already now? Here is the difficulty with lowering public debt. You cannot do it with a magic wand: there are economic costs to lowering public debt. There are political costs too, as the benefits from lowering public debt may become apparent only over time, and probably after the next election, while there may be costs in the short run. Thus the rest of this book looks at the costs of the various solutions available to lower public debt ratios and assesses them against the benefits of living in a lower public debt environment.

There are various ways to lower public debt. We will first consider some "shortcuts" that often attract quite a lot of attention because they promise to deliver a lower debt level at less pain with respect to orthodox fiscal adjustment. However, they also involve costs, and my view is that in most cases, these shortcuts are not as attractive as they seem to be, or simply are not feasible in practice under present circumstances. The first one is debt monetization, that is, printing money to repay debt. The second shortcut is financial repression, something that in the past was used quite frequently to facilitate the financing of governments and that may find new and unexpected variants in today's world. The third shortcut is defaulting on public debt and restructuring it, a sort of surgical operation that does not require too much time compared to regular fiscal adjustment. Many countries have done it, including, recently, Greece, although for the latter it has not really delivered as much as some had hoped (see chapter 11 for a discussion of Greece's situation). A fourth shortcut is the mutualization of debt, or the pooling of public debt among countries, something that has been considered for euro-zone countries and is technically possible but very unlikely to be feasible in practice. The fifth shortcut is to sell the crown jewels, that is, to privatize state assets, or at least raise their yield. It could work, if there just were enough assets to privatize, but there are not, unfortunately.

Finally, we will look at more orthodox solutions, which in my view are those that will lead in the current circumstances to the best results. The first is faster growth through the implementation of structural reforms. Faster growth is very important in lowering the public debt ratio because growth brings more revenue into the budget and because the denominator of the debt ratio rises faster. But structural reforms take time and need to be coupled with some degree of fiscal austerity, without going overboard but also without pretending that the debt problem can be solved without giving up something and without careful planning of the fiscal adjustment that would make it credible and sustainable over time. None of this will be easy. Any solution can only work though persistence over time. Stronger fiscal institutions and transparency can help in this respect. In any case, as Conan Doyle said, if you proceed by excluding impossible options (the shortcuts), whatever remains, no matter how improbable, must be the correct solution.

Part II

THE SHORTCUTS

SEVEN

Printing Money

The Bank of England, either by voluntarily discounting those bills at their current value, or by agreeing with government for certain considerations to circulate exchequer bills . . . keeps up their value and facilitates their circulation, and thereby frequently enables government to contract a very large debt of this kind. In France, where there is no bank, the state bills (billets d'etat) have sometimes sold at sixty and seventy per cent discount.

—*Adam Smith*

Printing money has been, over the centuries, a very common way of solving the sovereign's fiscal problems. As we have seen, to some extent, this is the solution that has been adopted so far, without major immediate drawbacks, as a large share of the recent increase in government debt has been financed by central banks. Will it work this time? And how would it work, if it does? This chapter looks at what monetary policy—basically, printing money—can do to help deal with public debt. We discussed this issue somewhat in earlier chapters but will now do so more comprehensively. We first consider what monetary policy can do to alleviate, for a time, the discomfort that high public debt can cause, and in this way reduce its immediate costs. We then look at what it can do through inflation to reduce public debt on a more stable basis, not just to alleviate the symptoms. And we look at the problems that can arise when monetary policy is executed in this fashion.

What Monetary Policy Can Do to Alleviate the Immediate Drawbacks of High Public Debt

Central banks can do a lot to alleviate the effects of high public debt in the short run. And they have done a lot. The issue is how long they can continue.

In chapters 1 and 2 we saw the main way in which central banks, by printing money, can help governments spend more than they collect in taxes. The difference (the deficit) can be bridged by borrowing not from private savers but from the central bank, primarily through the central bank's purchase of government securities. Public debt increases, but if the securities are held by the central bank, any interest paid to it goes back to the government, which receives its profits even in countries where the government formally does not own the central bank. In other words, the portion of public debt held by the central bank is not to be regarded as real debt, at least not in the immediate future. This is essentially what has happened to varying degrees in many advanced countries, which have continued to run sizable deficits since 2008.

Printing money has worked, at least in most cases, to keep interest rates on public debt low, even negative, and to reduce the risk of rollover crises caused by loss of confidence in the solvency of governments. Indeed, the 2011–12 wave of crises involved only advanced countries in the euro zone, countries that could not print money at will because they did not have their own central bank.

Central banks can help in another way, one that does not require printing money but just the possibility of printing money. As noted in chapter 3, when public debt is high, instances of what economists call "multiple equilibria" may arise: if interest rates start going up for whatever reason, the fiscal accounts look weaker and the default risk looks higher, prompting a new rise in interest rates, and so on until the fiscal accounts, which were sustainable at lower interest rates, become unsustainable at higher interest rates. Economists sometimes say these situations are exhibiting "self-fulfilling expectations." Many economists have noted that situations of multiple equilibria can be prevented if there is a central bank ready to monetize public debt. If the central bank stands ready to buy government paper by printing money, then the risk of not being repaid when the debt comes due disappears, and there is no point in speculating against government paper. The default risk premium disappears.

Have we solved the public debt problem? No, unfortunately. In economic history the printing of money by central banks to finance the government has typically been associated with a surge in inflation: more money is around, people start seeing it for what it is (a piece of paper, and, in modern times, an electronic record at the central bank), they try to get rid of it by buying real things (consumption goods or real assets), and this purchasing activity pushes up prices.

The relationship between printing money and inflation, however, is non-linear, which means that inflation can skyrocket suddenly. This happens when prices start going up not just because of an imbalance between the demand for and the supply of goods but because people get scared and start doubting the value, in terms of future purchasing power, of the pieces of paper we call money. Then they start buying anything at any price just to get rid of money, just to avoid holding paper that is losing its purchasing power. History is replete with well-documented inflationary outbursts of this sort, one of the most famous being the hyperinflation in Germany after World War I (the memory of that period still seems to make Germans fear inflation risk).[1]

And yet the risk of high inflation seems to be relatively remote now. What we have seen so far is really unprecedented. Central bank liabilities (base money) have more than doubled in the United States and almost quadrupled in Japan and the United Kingdom, and inflation is only now edging up and is still below the 2 percent level that many central banks regard as their target. The money that commercial banks hold as central bank deposits stays idle and does not generate more lending, economic activity, and inflation. Experts say that the transmission mechanism of monetary policy is not working as it did in the past. Why? And for how long can this situation last?

One view is that we are already feeling some of the effects of the increase in the money supply. Yes, consumer prices (the traditional measure of inflation) are not rising by much, but asset prices have been rising. Asset price bubbles caused by relaxed monetary conditions can be very dangerous: they eventually burst, which is what happened during the decade of the 2000s, when easy money contributed to triggering the 2008–09 global economic and financial crisis. That said, it remains a bit of a mystery why increases in the amount of base money of the magnitude we have seen since 2008 have not led, as in the past, to more standard forms of inflation. One can argue this has to do with globalization and the downward pressure it has created on wage growth. But the fact is, banks' liquidity does not really transmit to the rest of the economy. Could it be that banks do not lend more because borrowers are already too indebted in some countries or are simply too uncertain about the future to borrow more? Perhaps. Or perhaps banks' willingness to hold huge deposits at the central bank rather than lending has to do with banking regulations, leading to (perhaps unintended) forms of financial repression (see chapter 9). But no one really knows. We are in uncharted waters.

One scary scenario, however, is that at some point, all this money issued to finance public deficits will start being used, and very rapidly. One graphic way of picturing this situation is to visualize the money in the system as gasoline that has been funneled into a house. All feels normal—except for the bad odor—until someone lights a match. At present nobody is doing so, and things look fine. One should not be too alarmist about this possibility. If inflationary pressures arise, central banks stand ready to mop up the excess liquidity. Indeed, the Fed has now stopped increasing the money supply at a fast pace and has started raising interest rates. When monetary policy is tightened in earnest, however, even if the process proceeds in an orderly way, central banks will have to start selling on the market the government securities they have piled up (or will stop rolling over the maturing bonds), which will increase the pressure on government debt.

The bottom line is that, unless the rules of economics have fundamentally changed over the past ten years, unless for some structural reason (but I cannot think of any) banks become permanently willing to hold much larger amounts of base money in their portfolios than they used to, unless we believe that this time it's different, the noninflationary printing of money of the last few years has merely postponed the day of reckoning for governments. It is not a permanent solution. It alleviated the symptoms but did not remove the underlying problem.

Inflation as a Solution to the Public Debt Problem

If the fiscal accounts are not put under control, sooner or later their monetary financing will lead to inflation. Nobody really likes inflation, especially when it gets too high. Some studies show that inflation above 8 percent harms growth severely, and that it is better to stay far away from that threshold to avoid a slippery slope. Inflation, however, is not just a consequence of disorderly fiscal accounts. It can also work as a cure, and a cure that, despite its side effects, may still be regarded as preferable with respect to orthodox fiscal adjustment. How does inflation help bring down public debt? How much inflation is needed? Can inflation work in an orderly way without things getting out of hand?

The most important way in which inflation improves the fiscal accounts is by cutting the value in real terms (that is, in terms of purchasing power) of the public debt already in circulation issued at fixed interest rates.[2] Suppose I lend money to the government today by buying for $100 a twelve-month Treasury bill that bears a 2 percent interest rate. After one year, I get back $102, but the purchasing power of that $102 has declined by the amount of inflation in the period. For example, if inflation is 4 percent, I can buy fewer things with $102 after one year than I could have bought one year earlier with $100. I lose and the government gains (because in the meantime, its tax revenues have probably increased in line with inflation). This would not happen if the interest rate on the bill was indexed to inflation. But most government securities in circulation today were issued at fixed interest rates, and so their value in real terms can be eroded by inflation. This is the way public debt was dealt with after the first and second world wars in several countries, including Germany, Japan, and Italy. An inflation outburst quickly brought down public debt, my grandmother being one of the victims (she had unfortunately sold her land properties before the war to buy government paper, which was worthless after the war, even if it had never been repudiated).

How much inflation would be needed to make a sizable dent in the current stock of public debt in today's advanced economies? Here economists' opinions differ. Let's see why.

The key point to understand is that inflation can erode the value of bonds already in circulation, and investors will ask for higher interest rates on newly issued bonds if they perceive that inflation has increased. This is called the Fisher effect, after Irving Fisher, the economist who, early in the twentieth century, highlighted this mechanism. It implies that after a while, all bonds will have been issued at higher interest rates and their value will no longer be eroded by the higher level of inflation (unless inflation exceeds expectations). What definitely works in bringing down inflation is a rapid and violent surge in prices that does not give investors time to react, as happened after both world wars. But would a more moderate increase in inflation work? A study conducted when I was heading the Fiscal

Affairs Department of the International Monetary Fund (IMF) concluded that, if the Fisher effect is operating fully (which means that interest rates rise by as much as inflation), a moderate increase in inflation rates would not work: raising inflation to 6 percent for five years would not be very effective as it would reduce the public debt-to-GDP ratio by less than ten percentage points in the average of advanced economies, not much compared with public debt amounting to 100 percent of GDP or more.[3] To really make a difference, what would be needed is at least a surge of inflation to 25 percent for two years: then the debt would decline in the average of advanced economies by some thirty percentage points of GDP.

However, some prominent economists—among them Olivier Blanchard, with whom I had the pleasure of discussing this issue on a few occasions—are more optimistic as they believe that the Fisher effect would not hold, or in other words that interest rates would increase by less than inflation: interest rates on government debt would thus decline in terms of purchasing power. In my view such a favorable outcome would be unlikely to occur once conditions normalize, that is, once we emerge from the current situation in which people and banks are willing to hold large amounts of idle money balances at central banks. But remember that we are now considering a scenario in which inflation would be voluntarily used by central banks to reduce the public debt, and inflationary pressures would be rising. We are no longer in the environment of sleepy investors. To be fair, central banks could always keep interest rates as low as they wanted as long as they were willing to print enough money. But the perception that central banks were willing to print any amount of money to keep interest rates low would rapidly fuel inflationary expectations, so we would end up with an inflation burst, not with moderate inflation. Altogether, I am afraid the Fisher effect would hold, and there would have to be a sudden burst of inflation to lower public debt significantly, or, alternatively, some form of financial repression that would prevent interest rates from adjusting to inflation (see chapter 9).

There is another problem. Once the inflation genie is out of the bottle, it cannot be put back easily. It did happen after the two world wars: for example, in Italy, price stability was achieved during the second half of 1947. But it is probably easier to disinflate after a war as a new economic and often political regime is put in place. By contrast, it took a long time in many Latin American countries to get rid of inflation once inflation expectations became entrenched.

A final problem is that, when inflation has been persistently high for some time, the Fisher effect becomes perverse as interest rates start incorporating an inflation and devaluation premium. Turkey in the 1980s and 1990s experienced inflation rates close to 100 percent, mostly because of weaknesses in its fiscal accounts. The government had to pay nominal interest rates well above 100 percent (in some periods as high as 150 percent) because investors wanted to be compensated for the huge inflation and devaluation risk they were facing: they requested higher interest rates not only to reflect higher expected inflation but also to reflect the risks that the inflation rate could go even higher. This risk premium would therefore increase real interest rates. So, subjecting the central bank to the needs of fiscal policy (sometimes this is called "fiscal dominance") will reduce the default risk premium but can also create an inflation and devaluation premium, which can be equally damaging for the economy.

One last comment on the role of inflation in reducing public debt: when it works, it does so by eroding the value of government securities in circulation. It is a tax on bondholders like my grandmother (we return to this topic in chapter 10, which considers another form of tax on bondholders, outright default). So printing money is not really a painless solution, even from this point of view. Altogether, it does not seem to be the right solution.

EIGHT

First Case Study: Should European Countries Leave the Euro Zone?

The euro is our common fate, and Europe is our common future.

—Angela Merkel

The design of the "single-currency project" was so influenced by ideology and interests that it failed not only in its economic ambition, bringing prosperity, but also in its ambition of bringing countries closer together politically.

—Joseph E. Stiglitz

The role of monetary policy in euro-zone countries deserves a special discussion. Their central bank is the European Central Bank (ECB), whose statutory goal is to achieve an inflation rate of close to but below 2 percent. It is prohibited from financing directly the governments of member states but, like any other central bank, is allowed to buy securities issued by governments of the area if this is done not with the objective of financing them but of controlling the monetary conditions of the euro zone and in this way achieve the ECB inflation target. Of course, all this requires careful monetary management, and so it is not surprising that the ECB has moved relatively late in its program of quantitative easing, involving large increases in the money supply and purchases of government paper.

This delay in stepping into full action was strongly criticized by some economists earlier in the 2010s. For example, the Belgian economist Paul De Grauwe argued that the ECB should have started buying government paper much earlier to fight the multiple equilibria and "self-fulfilling expectations" that characterized the 2011–12 crisis.[1]

It was this dissatisfaction with the ECB—on top of the more general anti-European feelings that grew during this decade—that led some political parties in various European countries to call for an exit from the euro. Among other things, this would help solve the public debt problem, a point argued by, for example, two major political parties in Italy, the Five Star Movement and the Northern League.

Two reasons are usually adduced to explain why leaving the euro zone and reintroducing individual country currencies would help those countries' fiscal accounts. The first is that it would allow each country's central bank to intervene in support of the government paper market. The pros and cons of this approach were discussed in chapter 7, and there is little to add now, other than that avoiding inflation getting out of control would probably be even more difficult for a newly created currency, especially a currency that was created precisely to allow the printing of money to finance public deficits.

The second reason, however, deserves special attention and is somewhat more difficult to dismiss. It has to do with the alleged negative effects that the euro has had on the growth rate of some countries, including Italy.

Can Participation in the Euro Zone Harm Growth?

GDP growth is very important for debt sustainability, as more growth implies more government effective and potential revenues. Those who argue for an exit from the euro claim that the growth performance of some countries has been hampered by their participation in the euro zone. The euro, a strong currency, is good for some countries, such as Germany, but not for others, such as Italy, Portugal, and Spain.

Euro-skeptics include not only representatives of various political parties in Europe but also several economists. Indeed, many Nobel Prize laureates in economics—Paul Krugman, Joseph Stiglitz, Amartya Sen, Milton Friedman, James Mirrlees, Christopher Pissarides—have to a different extent expressed serious doubts about the viability of the euro project. With the exception of Friedman, all are economists toward the left of the political spectrum, who may identify the euro with the policies of fiscal austerity favored by Germany. But even supporters of fiscal discipline, such as the influential U.S. economist Martin Feldstein, expressed doubts about the euro as early as the mid-1990s, ahead of the euro's birth. So the anti-euro crowd is somewhat bipartisan. Is the criticism that participation in a common currency has hampered the growth of some countries in the euro zone justified? To be concrete, let's look at the specific case of Italy.

Since Italy joined the euro zone on January 1, 1999, its growth performance has been disappointing. Granted, Italy was not growing much in the 1990s, before the euro existed. However, until the end of the 1990s the Italian growth rate was lower only because population growth was lower: until then Italy's per capita income was rising more or less at the same pace as that of its European partners. Since 2001, soon after the introduction of the euro, things changed. Italy's per capita income (in real terms, that is, net of inflation) stopped rising and remained broadly constant until 2008. Thereafter it started declining, first with the global crisis of 2008–09 and then with the euro-zone crisis of 2011–12, whereas the per capita income of the rest of the euro zone rose steadily until 2008 and fell less rapidly thereafter. Only recently has Italy's income started rising again, but less rapidly than incomes elsewhere in Europe. In sum, Italy's per capita income, in terms of purchasing power, has dropped by more than 20 percent relative to per capita income in the rest of the euro zone since its entry into the euro zone.

Could it really be a coincidence that Italy's per capita income stopped growing soon after it joined the euro zone? Other developments may, of course, have affected Italy's growth rate. Italy is very dependent on oil imports, and oil prices rose from little more than $10 a barrel in 1998 to over $50 in 2005 and almost $100 in 2008. In general, commodity prices rose very fast during the last decade, and Italy is poor in commodities. Moreover, globalization—including the spectacular growth of exports from China and other new entrants into the global economy—may have hit Italy more severely than other countries because Italy's exports were more biased toward traditional goods (such as clothing), which were more subject to competition from low-wage countries. That said, sharing an exchange rate with countries less vulnerable to these developments at a minimum prevented Italy from responding to the commodity price and globalization shocks by depreciating its exchange rate to regain competitiveness. But let's look more closely at the reasons why adopting the euro may have hampered Italy's growth.

A first set of arguments used to explain why the euro is bad for the growth performance of some euro-zone countries is based on the theory of optimal currency areas. According to this theory, a necessary condition for a currency area to work well is that member countries have economic cycles that are relatively synchronized. What does that mean? We know that in some periods the economy of a country can grow faster and in other periods not as fast, and it may even experience a recession. This is what we call business cycles. Now, if the business cycles of the members of a currency area are synchronized (which means they are booming or regressing at more or less the same time), then the members can more easily share the same currency because the same monetary policy will be appropriate for all of them: lower interest rates and a more depreciated currency will be fine for everybody if they are all in a recession, while higher interest rates and a more appreciated currency will be good for everybody if they are all experiencing an economic boom and inflationary pressures. But if, for example, Italy is in a recession and Germany is in a boom, then the same monetary policy cannot be good for both countries, and each country would be better off with its own currency. The problem of asynchronous business cycles would be less severe if employment could move from the country that is in recession to the country that is booming. But labor mobility in Europe is low (at least it is lower than in the United States), and this strengthens the case of the euro-skeptics.[2]

This first argument against the euro does not seem particularly relevant from our perspective. What's really relevant for public debt sustainability is long-term growth, not the optimality of monetary policy during the ups and downs of economic cycles. Moreover, the growth problems of some countries in the euro zone are attributable not to cyclical shocks, which hit only some countries, but to more fundamental problems. These problems are indeed at the core of the current euro-zone debate: the business sector of Italy and some other euro-zone countries needs, structurally and not cyclically, a weaker currency to be competitive. The euro is a strong currency and essentially follows trends in productivity (how much a worker can produce in, say, one hour of work) in Germany and in the northern European countries. The Mediterranean countries have difficulty keeping up.

This is a much stronger argument, but we need to understand exactly what it implies. There is no reason why two countries with different productivity growth rates cannot share the same currency as long as wage developments in the two countries are consistent with the differences in productivity growth. What affects competitiveness is the cost of producing one unit of a product, which depends not only on how much is produced in one hour of work but also on how much one hour of work is paid. For example, if a worker in an Italian firm produces ten pencils per hour and a worker in a German firm produces twenty pencils per hour, the Italian firm can still be competitive if its workers are paid half the salary paid to German workers. In this case, the cost of labor per pencil produced—the unit labor cost—would be the same in both countries. This wage difference would indeed be justified by the lower productivity of Italian labor. Therefore, in itself, a lower productivity of Italian labor does not imply that the two countries cannot share the same currency. The same applies with respect to productivity growth: if productivity growth is higher in Germany than in Italy, Italy can be equally competitive as long as wages in Italy increase sufficiently less than wages in Germany.

The problem arises when wage increases are not in line with productivity increases. In this case, unit labor costs can rise more in one country than in another, and competitiveness may suffer from a labor cost differential. That is exactly what happened after the creation of the euro zone: unit labor costs (the labor cost of producing one pencil in the above example) in Italy and other southern European countries (Spain, Portugal, Greece), and to a lesser extent in France, have risen much faster than in Germany. Because prices could not increase as fast as unit labor costs, at least in the sectors exposed to foreign competition, as the exchange rate was fixed, profit margins were squeezed. But if profit margins are squeezed, firms invest less and economies grow less with less private investment. Altogether, these countries lost competitiveness relative to Germany.

The upward pressure on wages and prices was facilitated by the fast decline in interest rates that occurred in southern European countries after the euro zone was created. Because the currency was the same for all countries, markets stopped differentiating across countries in their investment decisions, which led to a broad convergence of euro-zone countries' interest rates. Their fast decline in southern European countries gave a temporary boost to those economies but also put pressure on wages and prices. What could have helped in that period would have been to cool down the economy by tightening fiscal policy sufficiently, which would also have had the additional benefit of fostering the convergence of public debt ratios with respect to Germany's. Unfortunately, that did not occur.

Taken together, all this meant that some euro-zone countries entered the euro zone unprepared to adjust their wage and price behaviors or their fiscal policies to a new world in which they could not periodically depreciate their currency to recover competitiveness. The problem had been anticipated. In May 1998 the governor of the Bank of Italy, Antonio Fazio, during the concluding remarks to his annual report—a highly publicized statement in Italy—argued that "adoption of the single European currency sets a lasting seal on monetary stability. It can be a source of growth, employment and sound public finances if economic policies and the behavior of the two sides of industry are compatible. Otherwise, it will lead to a loss of competitiveness, a weakening of the industrial fabric and an increase in unemployment."[3] These warnings were not heeded.

Once a competitiveness gap emerges, eliminating it is not easy if you cannot depreciate the exchange rate. It is not just a matter of avoiding future wage increases in line with productivity increases. It is also necessary to eliminate the productivity gap accumulated in the past (in the case of Italy, some 15 percent in terms of unit labor costs with respect to the average of euro-zone countries between 2000 and 2008 in the industrial sector).[4] This requires wages to grow less than productivity.

Does this mean that Italy and other southern European countries cannot go back to a robust growth path unless they leave the euro zone? Certainly not, though difficulties vary across countries, depending on the size of the competitiveness loss (for example, Greece by 2008 had lost 24 percent in terms of unit labor costs with respect to the euro-zone country average). Spain has already started regaining competitiveness: it had lost as much as Italy up to 2008, but then its unit labor costs started declining, and Spain is now growing at an annual rate of about 3 percent. Portugal is also recovering competitiveness. Structural reforms in the countries that need to catch up can facilitate the recovery of competitiveness as they can lead to faster productivity growth. So can cutting taxes on labor and profits, though they need to be financed by spending cuts to make their sustainability credible in high public debt countries. The fall in commodity prices that started in late 2014 will help countries such as Italy that depend more heavily on commodity imports. Finally, unit labor costs in Germany have been on the rise for a few years, which is also helping close the competitiveness gap.

One last important point must be clarified. Exiting the euro zone could perhaps lead to a faster recovery of competitiveness compared with a process based on containing wage increases with respect to productivity growth, essentially because in some countries it is difficult to cut wages in nominal terms. Exchange rate depreciation instead acts quickly. However, to work, the depreciation should not be followed by a rise in wages, so as to lower unit labor costs in terms of foreign currency and increase profit margins. So, while the adjustment speed may be different, it would still be necessary to contain wage growth in real terms. If a country remained in the euro zone, this would happen by containing nominal wages. If a country left the euro zone, this would happen through devaluation and inflation, which would also erode real wages. The end result would not look different in terms of real wages. This fact—that exiting the euro zone would allow a recovery of competitiveness only if the share of labor was reduced—is conveniently not emphasized by those in favor of an exit. And yet it is exactly what would happen.[5]

The Costs of Exiting the Euro Zone

Managing a euro-zone exit would be problematic. Wondering whether to adopt the euro is not the same thing as wondering whether to leave the euro-zone. A well-known problem in economics and in social sciences in general, one that economists refer to as "path dependence," is that our decision set is affected by where we are as a result of previous decisions. The most frequently quoted example is the QWERTY ordering of letters on our computer keyboard: the ordering is not the most rational one (a different ordering would minimize typing time), but it would be too costly to change it, and so keyboard manufacturers keep the ordering devised by Christopher Sholes in 1874 for mechanical typewriters, when the main concern was to avoid the jamming problems caused by the slow return of all parts of the typewriter to the rest position.

How costly would it be to leave the euro zone? The issue has never been explored in official published documents, for obvious reasons. The only public study I am aware of is one by the Swiss bank UBS, which concluded that the costs would be as high as 40 to 50 percent of GDP.[6] Others, such as the Italian euro-skeptic economist Alberto Bagnai in his book *Il tramonto dell'euro* (The sunset of the euro),[7] note that about seventy new currencies have been created since the end of World War II, and their creation has not given rise to any particular trouble. However, these cases include primarily the currencies of former colonies that gained political independence and not currencies emerging from the failure of a major economic integration project. Moreover, they included countries with fairly simple economic and financial systems, unlike the complex financial interrelationships that characterize the euro area. Altogether, I do not believe things would be so simple.

A euro-zone exit would also create immediate problems for public debt management. The public debt of euro-zone members is almost entirely denominated in euros. What would happen to it? There are two possibilities. The first is that the exiting countries would convert by law their euro debt into new currency debt at an arbitrary exchange rate. Then inflation and devaluation of the new currency would take care of eroding the value of public debt in real terms. The second possibility would be to maintain the euro denomination. In that case the debt service would rise heavily as the new currency would depreciate heavily against the euro (the depreciation would indeed be the very reason for leaving the euro zone). This rise would make it almost impossible to avoid a debt restructuring. Therefore, in both cases (conversions of debt into new lira and explicit debt restructuring) there would be a change in the terms of the bond contract and thus a technical default.[8] And a default gives rise to its own problems, discussed in chapter 10.

In conclusion, I do not think that leaving the euro zone offers an easy solution to the problems of high public debt and low growth. Of course, remaining in the euro zone without changing economic behavior and reforming the economy would be problematic. Perhaps the countries that lost competitiveness under the euro should have understood earlier that euro-zone entry required key changes in economic behavior. But I hope that the lesson has been learned. If not, there will be consequences.[9]

NINE

Financial Repression

History repeats itself, first as tragedy, second as farce.

—*Karl Marx*

A s we have seen, inflation by itself does not work to reduce public debt, unless it is so fierce that nobody really wants to try it. Moderate inflation would be more acceptable but would not work because interest rates on public debt would adjust to it, reducing considerably its effectiveness. Is there perhaps a way to prevent the adjustment of interest rates so that moderate inflation could have a chance? Could it be done, perhaps, by constraining investors to buy government paper at low interest rates? In a 2011 paper, Carmen Reinhart and M. Belen Sbrancia argue not only that this approach could work but also that this is how the problem of high public debt has often been solved over the past two centuries.[1] This chapter looks at how this strategy was executed in the past, how it is still being used in some emerging economies, and how it could work for advanced economies in the future. The chapter posits that, although in a form somewhat different from what Reinhart and Sbrancia were expecting, an "accidental financial repression" is, at present, at least allowing countries time to find more permanent solutions to the high public debt problem. How long this situation can last remains to be seen.

The Good Old Days of Financial Repression

There are many forms of financial repressions, but all share one feature: they prevent investors from doing what they want to do with their money. Financial repression often involves constraints on banks. The government, directly or through its central bank, can, for example, legally require banks to invest a certain share of their deposits in government securities. This requirement tends to lower the interest rate on government paper. Or the government can set a cap on bank lending to the private sector, which also tends to move bank portfolios toward investing in government bonds. Or it can cap deposit rates, which lowers the cost of funding for banks and, indirectly, the government's cost of borrowing from banks. Constraints can also be imposed on nonbank investors. For example, the government can constrain the possibility, for any resident, of investing money abroad. This forces savers to invest in domestic assets, including government paper.

All these maneuvers worked pretty well in the past, and in fact were quite common in most advanced economies until the 1980s. For example, until the 1980s Italy had bond investment requirements for banks, as well as ceilings on bank lending; regulation Q constrained bank deposit rates in the United States in the post–World War II period (though it started losing effectiveness being circumvented in the 1970s and 1980s); and most advanced economies had constraints on investing abroad until the 1980s.

When investment opportunities are limited by financial repression, it becomes easier for inflation to erode the value of public debt in real terms. Even moderate inflation can do so as nominal interest rates will not take fully into account the level of inflation, and real interest rates on public debt will be lower than they would otherwise be. Reinhart and Sbrancia note that many historical episodes of a gradual reduction in public debt were at least facilitated by financial repression, including in the post–World War II period, essentially because financial repression succeeded in keeping real interest rates low and sometimes negative. Reinhart and

Sbrancia estimate that financial repression had a major impact on the fiscal accounts of economically advanced countries in the post–World War II period:

> For the United States and the United Kingdom our estimates of the annual liquidation of debt via negative real interest rates amounted on average from 3 to 4 percent of GDP a year. For Australia and Italy, which recorded higher inflation rates, the liquidation effect was larger (around 5 percent per annum).

These good old days seemed to have gone. The process of financial liberalization that started during the 1980s and was virtually completed in many advanced economies during the 1990s involved the removal of most financial repression tools. The process was prompted by the recognition that financial repression prevented money from going where market forces were leading it, which made economies less efficient. If money is channeled into government securities, it is not available to finance private investment, even when the latter would be economically justified and could perhaps enhance the economy's welfare more than government spending could. If you believe market forces should be allowed to operate, then investment decisions should not be constrained. I am not saying that all that I have described is completely and always true, but, whether you like it or not, the pro-market mood of the 1980s and the 1990s led to the almost complete removal of financial repression tools in advanced economies.

But the same did not happen elsewhere, at least not to the same degree. India, for example, still constrains Indian residents' ability to invest abroad, and also caps some interest rates. These measures have helped to lower interest rates on government paper, which have often been negative in real terms. As a result, the level of public debt in India, though high for emerging economies, is not as high as it would have been otherwise, in the context of India's large imbalance between government revenues and primary government spending.[2]

Those days seemed to be gone for advanced economies, but then things changed in the aftermath of the 2008–09 global financial crisis. But history never repeats itself fully, so financial repression returned, if not as a farce, as Karl Marx might have predicted, at least in a different form and with different implications for public finances.

The Accidental Financial Repression

A large share of the fiscal deficits that emerged after 2007 in advanced economies was to a large extent financed by printing money (see chapter 2). This money ended up in banks, which gladly hold it in deposits in central banks at interest rates that currently are low to negative. Why do they do it? Why don't they lend that money to the business sector? Or to households? And, with respect to the whole economy, why did all this money printing not lead to a surge in inflation?

The standard answer is that there is not much demand for bank lending, partly because, as a result of the financial liberalization of the 1980s and the 1990s and the global recession of 2008–09, business and households have already borrowed too much and are now trying to reduce their debt. But this cannot be the whole story as often one hears about many (especially small and medium-sized) enterprises that simply cannot get enough credit from banks. A different explanation—it may not be the whole story, but it could be part of the story—is that banks are unwilling or, better, unable to lend because they do not have enough equity. Bank equity is essentially bank's own money, the resources that they do not borrow: it is the capital that the bank shareholders invest in the banking business. What is constraining credit and money growth is not the lack of liquidity—banks have plenty of it, deposited at central banks. They lack bank equity. Bank equity is needed to increase bank lending. Banks can have a lot of borrowed money in their portfolios, but if they do not have enough equity, bank regulations prevent them from lending it. These regulations aim at avoiding a situation in which banks assume too much risk using borrowed money, and they have been tightened in the aftermath of the 2008–09 global financial crisis.

The 2008–09 financial crisis revealed that banks and other financial intermediaries, which could now behave more freely after the financial deregulation of the 1980s and 1990s, loved risk a bit too much. And they loved assuming risk using borrowed money, other people's money. As a result, governments and central banks are now rightly asking banks to have much more own money with respect to the money they borrow: the bank equity requirements have been sharply raised. Today, if a bank wants to increase lending to the private sector, it needs to raise much more equity than it had to before the 2008–09 crisis. The same is not true if instead a bank wants to lend to the government by buying government securities because government securities are regarded as risk-free and have a zero weight in the formula used to assess how much equity a bank needs to have. This tightening of equity regulations was decided not just in one or two countries. It was a decision made under the aegis of the Basel Committee, which coordinates bank supervision decisions across the world.[3] All this was right, but it constrained the growth of bank lending.

The problem related to the scarcity of bank equity is exacerbated by two factors. The first is the uncertainty about future regulatory changes that may involve additional increases in bank equity: we have recently heard about the major objections that the banking community is raising to a further tightening of equity requirements that could arise from a new round of bank regulation decisions (sometimes called "Basel 3.5" or "Basel 4," following previous rounds of Basel agreements). This uncertainty makes banks even more prudent in lending money because they fear finding themselves short of capital if the requirements on the latter are raised further. The second factor is a direct consequence of the expansionary monetary policies of the last few years. The low interest rates they brought about reduced the profitability of banks, and this situation makes it harder to attract new equity.[4]

Let's recap. Central banks print money to finance the government deficit, the money ends up in commercial banks and is deposited at the central bank, and banks cannot lend it to the private sector because they do not have enough equity. So the money stays in the central bank. That is not entirely good for the government because the economy does not grow very much with limited bank lending. And with low economic activity, it is also difficult to raise inflation to those moderate levels that would help erode the stock of public debt in real terms. This is not quite what happened in the golden days of financial repression, as described by Reinhart and Sbrancia. But the situation is not terrible either: it helps by postponing the day of reckoning for the government. Interest rates on public debt stay low, and there is no risk that inflation will get out of control.

I do not think that the current combination of super-relaxed monetary policies and a tightening of bank equity regulation was intended to help finance the government through financial repression. I do not think there was an evil master plan. The financial repression is probably fully accidental. The tightening of capital requirements was a natural reaction to the financial excesses of the pre-2008 period that led to the 2008–09 crisis. And the monetary policy relaxation is consistent, in the presence of regulatory tightening and the current moderation in economic growth, with the mandate of central banks to keep inflation close to its target, which is now being undershot in many countries. But the combination of relaxed monetary policy and relaxed bank regulations is nonetheless quite effective in making, at least for the moment, public debt sustainable at very low interest rates, and thus is greatly benefiting the fiscal accounts.

Once again, we have to ask: How long will it last? Will banks at one point undertake activities to get rid of excess liquidity in ways that do not absorb equity, such as by purchasing foreign government paper or currency, with potentially destabilizing effects on foreign exchange markets? How soon will equity start flowing again in sufficient amounts to banks? (Equity requirements cannot be raised forever, and the banking community is already complaining.) How soon will lending accelerate to the point that inflation reaches unpleasant levels? (As described in chapter 8, this is not a desirable outcome.) When that happens, will more traditional, full-fledged financial repression tools be reintroduced? Could banks again be forced openly to buy government paper? (That would not be great either. After all, we agreed that preventing money from going where market forces would lead it was not good for the economy.) Perhaps the right thing to do if inflationary pressures eventually materialize would be to mop up gradually the huge liquidity created by central banks to finance the government, with the support of fiscal adjustment, as discussed in Part III of this book. That might be the right thing to do. But we are not there yet. We still need to consider other, less orthodox forms of public debt reduction. The next chapter talks about the surgical cure of defaulting on government debt.

TEN

Default

When national debts have once been accumulated to a certain degree, there is scarce, I believe, a single instance of their having been fairly and completely paid. The liberation of the public revenue, if it has ever been brought about at all, has always been brought about by bankruptcy.

—Adam Smith

If you become seriously ill, you can take drugs and wait a period of time for them to take effect. Or, depending on your condition, you may choose to undergo surgery. Surgery is painful and risky. People try to avoid it if they can. But it is fast. And sometimes it is inevitable. Declaring bankruptcy, defaulting on government debt, is like surgery. It gets rid of the public debt disease quickly. It may be a difficult decision to make, but once made there is no turning back. Slow-moving cures—gradual fiscal adjustments of the kind to be discussed in chapter 15—take time, require a persistent commitment, and are exposed to the risk of "reform fatigue," as economists sometimes call it. I believe that is why many economists like the default solution, over and beyond purely economic factors.

Moreover, defaulting on public debt is something that appeals instinctively to those who dislike financial markets and the fiscal austerity they sometimes impose (to be repaid) through their henchman, the International Monetary Fund (IMF). David Graeber, one of the founders of the Occupy Wall Street movement, writes that "the International Monetary

Fund [acts] as the world's debt enforcer. . . . You may say, the high-finance equivalent of the guys who come to break your legs."[1] Defaulting on public debt instead is presented as an alternative to fiscal austerity. It seems to avoid the need to raise taxes or to cut spending. It seemingly allows larger fiscal deficits and more support of economic activity, more Keynesian policies. The political left, or part of it, also likes it for these reasons.

But does defaulting on public debt really render other hard choices unnecessary? This chapter argues that it does not, that there are sizable costs associated with defaulting on public debt, that it does not remove the need for fiscal austerity, that it is not necessarily pro-growth, that it may not hit primarily the rich, and, perhaps to the surprise of many, including David Graeber, that the IMF does not oppose debt restructuring. On the contrary, the IMF increasingly requires debt restructuring as a condition for receiving loans.

A Brief History of Debt Repudiation

There are many forms of debt repudiation. The term is used in general to refer to any form of change in the terms of the contract underlying the issuance of government paper.[2] The government may decide to reduce the interest rate it pays, to increase the maturity of the bond (which means paying later than promised), or to repay only part of the principal, in which case we talk about the government applying a "haircut" to its bonds. The process that leads to debt repudiation often begins with the government missing one debt service payment, for example the payment of a maturing coupon. This causes what technically is called a *default*. It means the government has a problem in servicing its debt, and at that point (though it can also happen earlier), long and often complex negotiations are initiated between the government and its creditors, whose number can be very large in the case of debt issued in the form of marketable bonds. But we are not interested in these details. In what follows, I will use the expressions "debt repudiation," "debt restructuring," and "debt default" synonymously to mean any change in the terms on which the government debt was originally contracted, regardless of the specific way in which the change occurs.

Government debt defaults are quite common, especially in emerging economies. Carmen Reinhart and Ken Rogoff, in their book *This Time Is Different: Eight Centuries of Financial Folly*, tell us that, since the beginning

of the nineteenth century, there have been more than 320 cases of debt repudiation in the sixty-six countries considered by them, or an average of
more than one per year.[3] Debt repudiation, however, occurs in waves: defaults occur more frequently in periods of economic crisis of the countries
involved, when government revenues decline and public deficits and debt
rise; and economic crises do come in waves, affecting many countries at
the same time, because the crises arise from common shocks and contagion effects (contagion means that investors may run away from countries
with similar economic and financial features).

If we look more closely at the composition of debt repudiation episodes,
two things stand out. The first is that, of the more than 320 cases of default, only seventy concern domestic debt, which confirms what was stated
in chapters 1 and 3, namely, that repudiating domestic debt is much more
unpleasant than repudiating external debt because domestic debt hits domestic residents and voters. The second interesting thing is that, after
World War II, debt repudiation in advanced economies has been very rare.
Before World War II several of the countries that now are considered among
the advanced economies had undertaken various forms of debt restructuring. For example, in 1933 the United States eliminated from some of its
bond contracts the clause that allowed creditors to be repaid in gold. During the nineteenth century the United Kingdom on several occasions
reduced the interest rate on bonds already in circulation, and in 1932 it
lowered the interest rate on the debt issued during World War I. However,
after the war no advanced economy had ever repudiated its public debt
before Greece did so at the end of 2011.[4] These two things are related: public debt in emerging economies is often primarily external debt, or at least
it was so in the past, because the domestic financial markets of emerging
economies are underdeveloped, and therefore these countries are more
likely to repudiate their public debt.

Debt Restructuring in Advanced Economies

Even if in the last few decades public debt restructuring has, with one exception, not been used by advanced economies, the recent surge in public
debt has led many to believe that, sooner or later, some other economies
will follow Greece's example, particularly among the euro-zone countries,

where alternative solutions such as monetizing debt are less viable. The supporters of debt restructuring include both politicians and economists.

Italy is a case in point. When it comes to political forces, debt repudiation is advocated as a solution to the high-debt problem by one of the largest political parties, Beppe Grillo's Five Star Movement, even if recently the movement has placed greater stress on leaving the euro zone as the way forward (but, as we have seen, leaving the euro zone would almost certainly require public debt restructuring). Public debt restructuring is also advocated by some of the political groups to the left of Italy's Democratic Party.

As for economists, many have argued that, given the difficulties in implementing fiscal adjustment when an economy is not growing fast, Italy and other southern European countries such as Portugal, and perhaps more, will have to restructure their debt. This view has been expressed, for example, by some former IMF staff members (Desmond Lachman, now at the America Enterprise Institute, and Ashoka Mody, now at Princeton), as well as by Willem Buiter, currently chief economist of Citigroup.[5] The same view was taken by Peter Boone and Simon Johnson (a former IMF chief economist) in a paper written in 2012, in the midst of the euro-zone crisis, and by one of the most followed commentators on international economic issues, Nouriel Roubini, who, at the height of the euro-zone crisis, argued that "it is increasingly clear that Italy's public debt is unsustainable and needs an orderly restructuring to avert a disorderly default."[6]

Would it be a good idea for some high-debt advanced economies to restructure their public debt? One could argue first that countries do not necessarily choose to restructure their debt. They may be forced by investors to do so. If investors stop lending to a country because they believe the risk of not being repaid is too high, a government will have no alternative to stop servicing its debt, particularly if the amount of debt coming to maturity every week or every month is so large that sufficient financial resources to repay it are unavailable (short of stopping paying salaries, pensions, and so forth suddenly and just using any available tax revenues to repay the maturing debt).

The question we are considering here, however, is a bit different: Should governments of high-debt countries strategically decide to restructure their debt? Would they be better off with respect to other approaches to lowering public debt? Those who call for a strategic debt restructuring see two main advantages to this option. The first is that debt restructuring would avoid the alternative path to debt reduction, fiscal austerity, which would be bad for the economy as it would have recessionary effects. The second advantage is that the burden of debt restructuring would be borne by the bondholders, who are wealthy, and therefore from an income distribution and equity perspective would be preferable to fiscal austerity, which would always end up hitting more the needy. But does debt restructuring really deliver a less austere, more equitable fiscal adjustment? Let's start with the question of austerity.

Does Debt Restructuring Really Mean Less Fiscal Austerity?

I have some doubts. The costs of fiscal austerity, in my view, are sustainable as long as austerity is implemented with a grain of salt, is gradual, and is accompanied by structural reforms to improve the growth potential of advanced economies (see chapter 15). The costs of debt restructuring, however, including costs in the form of the austerity it brings about, are largely underestimated by supporters of debt restructuring.

Economists know well that debt restructuring involves some costs. The cost that has been studied more closely is the loss of reputation associated with debt restructuring. If I lend you some money today and after a while you tell me that you cannot pay me back in full, next time you ask me for a loan either I will simply say no or I will ask for a higher interest rate to compensate me for the higher risk I have to sustain now that you have lost your reputation as a trustworthy borrower. These reputational costs have been studied extensively, and some economists have concluded that they are not so high. Granted, Argentina, which repudiated its debt in 2001, has only recently been able to reenter international capital markets, but on average, countries seem able to go back to financial markets relatively quickly after a debt repudiation—two or three years after, as estimated by Eduardo Borensztein and Ugo Panizza.[7] In other words, financial markets suffer from short-term memory. However, recent work by Juan J. Cruces and Christopher Trebesch reaches a different conclusion: reputational costs are high if the haircut is large.[8] In other words, markets forget quickly unless they are badly hurt.

Be that as it may, reputational costs are only part of the costs sustained by a country that repudiates its debt. There are indeed direct costs that an economy suffers as a result of the fiscal austerity that accompanies a debt restructuring. Fiscal austerity? But wasn't debt restructuring an alternative to fiscal austerity? Not really. Debt restructuring is like a tax, but instead of taxing income or wealth, the government taxes one specific form of wealth, that invested in government securities. Debt restructuring is equivalent to taxing the bondholders. In other words, debt restructuring is just one form of fiscal adjustment, one form of austerity, not a substitute for fiscal adjustment.[9]

Now, if the bondholders are foreign investors, living perhaps thousands of miles away, we need not worry too much about the economic consequences of the fiscal tightening arising from debt restructuring, as it will hit other countries. This was the case, for example, with the debt restructuring operations undertaken by some Latin American countries in the 1980s: the main creditors were U.S. banks, and their losses did not have any substantial spillover effects on the defaulting countries. Things are currently very different for most advanced economies.

The most obvious example is Italy. Sixty percent of Italian public debt is currently held by Italian banks, insurance companies, households, and other residents. Therefore, debt restructuring would mean taxing by and large Italian residents, and such a tax, like any other tax, would have an impact on aggregate demand: those who are taxed would have a lower capacity to spend. One could say that a debt restructuring, for example a haircut, does not require bondholders to pay anything, and therefore it does not have an impact on the liquidity and spending capacity of anyone. But that is not really the case, as the debt service payments for interest payments and debt redemption would be directly lowered. There is therefore no reason to believe that the default tax (let's call it what it is) would have no austerity effect. By the way, the default tax would be fully frontloaded and thus would hit bondholders quite violently. The issue is further complicated by the fact that a large share of government bonds is often held by domestic banks, which would be directly hit in terms of liquidity and capitalization if public debt were restructured.[10] Thus banks would have to be somehow sheltered from the debt restructuring in order to avoid deposit runs and a full banking crisis, but this would reduce the beneficial impact of the restructuring for the fiscal accounts or would require even larger haircuts for other investors.[11]

One could argue that, in part, the default tax would be paid by foreign bondholders. That's true, but in many cases it would not mean an absence of major consequences for the defaulting country. Countries in the euro zone, for example, are quite integrated with one another. A default by one would have direct consequences for the others, not least as holders of government paper issued by the defaulting country.

In terms of impact on the financial markets, one has to take into account also the sheer magnitude, in absolute terms and not just in percent of GDP, of the debt of some of the high-debt advanced economies. It is one thing to restructure the public debt of Uruguay, Ukraine, or even Greece, the impact of which could be absorbed relatively easily by financial markets. It would be an entirely different matter if, say, Italy had to restructure its public debt, which is, in euro terms, almost seven times the size of Greece's debt when the latter was restructured, a point effectively made by Adair Turner, former head of the U.K. Financial Stability Authority, in his book *Between Debt and the Devil*.[12] There would be severe consequences for the entire world, with huge spillover effects on Italy. We do not even want to think about the consequences of a default of U.S. government debt.

There is, however, one aspect that makes many lean toward the default tax solution: as noted at the beginning of this chapter, it is like surgery. It is quick. It requires resolve, but not a prolonged commitment. As people say about smoking, if you want to stop, you have to stop altogether, not try to do so gradually. Many people love this "cold turkey" approach. By contrast, lowering public debt by sustaining over time a sizable primary surplus requires a prolonged effort, which may not be politically sustainable over time. It's better to be bold and make the difficult decision that will solve the debt problem for good. This approach to fiscal adjustment is appealing to many economists. But, leaving aside the dubious psychological advantages, there is a seemingly strong economic rationale to an upfront, large cut in public debt: it is a one-off operation, and as such it does not alter future economic incentives and decisions. By contrast, maintaining a large primary surplus over time means, for example, keeping higher taxes on labor, thus discouraging labor supply, or on profits, thus discouraging private investment. This advantage with respect to orthodox fiscal adjustment depends on whether it is possible to increase the primary surplus without undermining in a major way the growth potential of the economy, which perhaps could be done if a government was able to identify, for example, forms of wasteful spending (discussed in chapter 15). Moreover, the argument is also based on the assumption that the restructuring really is a one-off event, which would require an even larger default tax.

If the cold turkey approach is really preferred, then it is not clear why only wealth held in the form of domestic government bonds should be taxed. Why not taxing the whole of wealth rather than a specific form of wealth? A tax on wealth would be spread over a larger base and thus would require a lower tax rate. And taxing those who invested in domestic government paper seems unfair on the face of it: it would penalize investors who trusted the government and reward those who preferred investing abroad. This is connected to the broader issue of the fairness of a default tax, to which we now turn.

Who Would Pay the Default Tax?

Those who argue in favor of debt restructuring believe it would primarily affect the rich (including the banks) and that the burden of orthodox austerity measures would fall primarily on the poor. Whether this is really the case is debatable. Little or no work has ever been done on the redistributional effects of public debt restructuring. Moreover, whether debt restructuring is more or less favorable to the poor by comparison with orthodox fiscal adjustment depends on how the orthodox fiscal adjustment is implemented: some austerity policies can affect the wealthy more than the poor.

Let's clarify a couple of points. First, behind financial intermediaries, which often hold large amounts of government paper, there are many small depositors, and certainly not all of them are wealthy. Second, the wealthy typically hold a lower share of their wealth invested in government bonds. Information available on the direct holdings of government paper shows that the relatively rich hold more government bonds than the relatively poor. This is clear, for example, from data published for Italy by the Bank of Italy, based on surveys of households' portfolios. But the same survey also shows that all forms of financial wealth are held in larger proportions by the rich, quite obviously. However, for the relatively well-off, the share of wealth invested in government bonds in Italy is somewhat lower than the share of wealth invested in other forms of wealth, relative to the distribution of wealth of the less well-off. For example, the less well-off do not invest in sophisticated financial instruments. This confirms that, if you really want to tax wealth, a tax on all forms of wealth would be more equitable than a default tax.

The Views of the IMF on Debt Restructuring

Let me close this chapter by clarifying the views of the IMF on debt restructuring. It is not at all true that the IMF rules out debt restructuring as a fiscal adjustment tool when public debt is too high. On the contrary, my view is that, if anything, now the IMF is pushing for debt restructuring sometimes with too much energy, disregarding that debt restructuring could perhaps have more severe effects on a country's economy than gradual fiscal adjustment.

There is no doubt that, in a fairly remote past, the IMF regarded debt repudiation as a measure of last resort for an indebted country. But things changed. Already in the 1980s debt restructuring was a key component of IMF-supported programs, especially those undertaken by Latin American countries. Toward the end of the 1990s, the IMF formally introduced a policy of "private sector involvement" based on a clear appreciation of the benefits that debt restructuring can—in some cases—have.[13] Among other things, the IMF noted that debt restructuring helps avoid moral hazard by lenders, or the tendency of investors to lend irresponsibly to countries that are unable to repay the debt and that count on the IMF to step in and bail them out again if things get sour. It is a reasonable concern: if, in agreeing to lend to a country at risk, I request a higher interest rate as a compensation for that risk, why should I be repaid fully through IMF money, should the debtor get in trouble? If I were repaid in such a fashion, I would be encouraged to assume too much risk, making financial crises more likely. Moreover, from a fairness perspective, why should IMF money be used to repay investors who profited through the high interest rates they received from lending to countries in trouble? The IMF has often been accused—especially by the America political right—of bailing out private investors. Now it seems to have learned its lesson and is much more favorable to bailing in through debt restructuring.

These are valid arguments, and over the past few years the IMF has introduced increasingly sophisticated ways of assessing public debt sustainability, focusing also on whether the fiscal tightening needed to restore fiscal sustainability would be consistent with economic growth. And, more often than in the past, the IMF has come to the conclusion that debt restructuring is preferable to an orthodox fiscal adjustment (of relevance to this discussion, the IMF's current views on Greece are discussed in chapter 11).

All this is fine, but now the IMF may be going too far in the opposite direction, ignoring the costs of debt restructuring, including the recessionary costs associated with it. It is indeed surprising that the main document that provides instructions to the IMF staff on how to assess public debt sustainability does not even mention the need to evaluate the costs of a debt restructuring in terms of growth and how those costs compare with the costs of orthodox fiscal adjustment, as if the former did not exist.[14] The IMF often talks about the need for orderly debt restructuring and, in the face of evidence that debt restructuring is often messy and does not yield the expected results, as in the case of Greece, has often taken the view that this is because the debt restructuring was unnecessarily delayed. Of course, it is impossible to have a counterfactual, so it is always safe to argue that if restructuring had been done earlier, things would have turned out differently. And yet from the fact that debt restructuring did not work it does not follow that it would have worked better had it been implemented earlier. The burden of proof falls on debt restructuring believers.

One final clarification of the position of the IMF: you may be wondering why the IMF, which is often a creditor of countries in trouble, would be inclined to support debt restructuring operations that penalize creditors. This point is less surprising once you know that the IMF enjoys a "preferred creditor status," which means that debt restructuring never involves IMF loans. Only other creditors are penalized by a debt restructuring, and in fact, the cancellation of debt owed to other creditors makes it more likely that the IMF will be repaid. Indeed, over the more than seventy years of its existence the IMF has virtually lost no money from its lending activities. The IMF almost always gets repaid, which, among other things, tells you that the bailing-out argument (private investors are bailed out by IMF's international taxpayers' money) is flawed. Private investors eventually return to a country, even if they may initially be refunded through IMF resources, and all the international taxpayers' money is eventually repaid.

ELEVEN

Second Case Study: The Greek Crisis

To hear Germany's critics, one would think that the word and the concept of "austerity" was a dubious Teutonic gift to the world. In fact, *Austerität* is rarely used in German. It was borrowed fairly recently from English, which got it from French. The French got it from Latin, and the Romans took it from, of all sources, Greek: *austeros* means bitter.

—The Economist, *July 18, 2015*

The history of the Greek economic crisis that started in 2009 and is still unfolding goes well beyond the issue of Greek public debt. It is also the history of deep tensions between northern and southern Europe and of the persistent controversy over how the euro area should work. But the debate about the sustainability of Greek public debt, about the severe debt restructuring that took place in 2011, and about the remaining need for additional debt restructuring, this time of the debt held by Greece's official European creditors, has been at the core of the contention. Thus, discussing the Greek crisis will allow us to better focus some of the arguments introduced in the previous chapter.

The Origin of the Crisis

Greek GDP (in real terms, that is, net of inflation) contracted between 2008 and 2013 by almost a quarter. In the same period the unemployment rate almost quadrupled, to over 27 percent. These figures well describe the depth of the Greek crisis. Economic conditions improved a bit in 2014 but, following a new political crisis, started weakening again in 2015, and only recently seem to have stabilized.

What caused the crisis? Was it caused by the austerity policies imposed by the troika (the name given to the three institutions, the European Commission, the European Central Bank, and the International Monetary Fund [IMF] that coordinated the economic support package granted to Greece in exchange for fiscal and structural adjustment)? How responsible are the Greek governments that, in rapid succession, have been in power during the last few years? Unfortunately, many mistakes were made, and by more than one side. Let's start from the beginning.

Greece reached the eve of the global economic crisis of 2008–09 after a prolonged if unsustainable economic boom, something that is not usually underscored. Real GDP increased at an average annual rate of 4 percent between 1998 and 2007, a cumulative increase of 42 percent. This means that, despite the decline in GDP in the following period, Greece's GDP today still exceeds the 1999 level, Greece thus faring not too badly by comparison with other southern European countries (Italy's GDP is currently close to the 1999 level, the country having experienced a milder drop in GDP than Greece after 2008 but also much lower growth before 2008).

The pre-2008 economic boom had been caused by Greece's entry into the euro zone and by the related fast drop in interest rates at which Greek households, firms, and the government could borrow. In a common monetary area, interest rates tend to converge to a common level as investors tend to move from countries with lower interest rates to countries that, before the entry into the common area, had higher interest rates. This happens as long as there are no concerns about the sustainability of the common currency area, and there were no concerns when the euro was introduced. European banks felt confident in lending to Greece at low interest rates. That meant that, during most of the 2000s, European banks, as well as private citizens, through the purchase of Greek securities, financed, at fairly low interest rates, a spectacular rise in spending by Greek households, firms, and government. GDP was boosted by this increased spending as the demand for domestic products was also rising, especially for nontradable services. However, spending by Greek residents was rising faster than Greek GDP, and so imports were also rising faster.

Greek imports of goods and services almost tripled between 1998 and 2007, an increase of almost €50 billion. Exports could not keep up with this increase, especially in euro terms, penalized by a rise in labor costs that, as in other southern European countries, were rising faster than in Germany (see chapter 8). But the acceleration in Greek unit labor costs was much faster than in any other euro-zone country. As a consequence of the widening gap between import and export growth, Greece's external position became more and more unbalanced. The imbalance between imports and exports (the *external current account deficit*) approached 15 percent of GDP in 2008. It was as if a household's income was $100 and the household was spending $115, year after year. By sustaining an imbalance, Greece was rapidly accumulating public and private debt toward the rest of the world, particularly Europe.

All this means that, in the run-up to the crisis, international savers (even when the direct lending comes through banks, the resources ultimately come from German, Italian, or French savers) were financing spending by Greek residents. The spending was fueling European exports to Greece, which was good for employment outside Greece. But ultimately the German or Italian or French worker was producing for the benefit of the Greek consumer and receiving in exchange a lot of IOUs. The surge in Greece's external debt would have been more sustainable if it had financed productive investments. Unfortunately, it was financing consumption and low-quality investment.

Higher spending by Greek residents was fueled not only by declining interest rates but also by public spending. In 2008 the fiscal deficit was equal to 10 percent of GDP, well above the 3 percent ceiling envisaged by European fiscal rules. Such a sizable deficit was even more worrisome because it was following a prolonged economic boom. When the economy grows rapidly, government revenues also rise faster (or at least they should), and if spending is kept under control, the fiscal deficit should decline. This did not happen in the case of Greece. In 2008 Greek public debt was equal to 107 percent of GDP. How was all this possible without running afoul of the ironclad European fiscal rules? Well, at that time the European fiscal rules were not as ironclad as they are now (though even now they are not as ironclad as many believe; see chapter 16). Moreover, the data made available by the Greek authorities on its fiscal accounts were rigged.

Rigged Data

The European Commission knew very well that the Greek fiscal deficit was exceeding the 3 percent of GDP threshold and, until mid-2007, Greece was subject to an "excessive deficit procedure," the procedure that applies to euro-zone countries with deficits exceeding the threshold that could lead to financial sanctions. But in 2007 the procedure was terminated because available data showed that the fiscal deficit had declined below 3 percent. However, the procedure was restarted in 2008 because the data provided by the Greek government again showed a deficit above 3 percent.

The official deficit data, however, largely underestimated the deficit. In its annual report on Greece in mid-2009 the IMF expressed concern for the statistical discrepancies between the official deficit data and other statistical data, in particular the data on the government cash flow and the securities issued by the government, which suggested that the deficit was larger than reported. Indeed, in October 2009 the new Greek government acknowledged that the fiscal deficit, as well as the public debt data, published until then were just wrong. The 2008 deficit was as high as 7.7 percent of GDP, not 5 percent of GDP. (The deficit was later further revised, up to 10 percent of GDP.) The public debt amounted to 115 percent of GDP, not 100 percent as previously stated.

Once the true state of Greece's fiscal accounts became known, financing to Greece rapidly dried up. Greece lost access to financial markets and had to ask for help from the European partners and the IMF. But the realization that Greece had lied in the data it had provided both to Europe and to the IMF undermined from the beginning the confidence that should exist among international partners. Granted, the rigged data had been provided by the previous government, but those developments revived feelings of mistrust that were thousands of years old, well epitomized by Virgil's "Timeo Danaos et dona ferentes" (I do not trust the Greeks even bearing gifts). You cannot trust the Greeks, and perhaps other Mediterranean people (Germany's Volkswagen scandal was still far in the future).[1] Altogether the first financing package to support Greece's adjustment program did not start propitiously.

The Failure of the First Financing Program Extended to Greece

The adjustment and financing program agreed to by Greece on one side, and the IMF and the European countries on the other, in May 2010 envisaged, in addition to important structural reforms, a massive dose of fiscal austerity, with the goal of lowering the fiscal deficit below 3 percent of GDP by 2014: the deficit was targeted to decline by 5.5 percentage points of GDP between 2009 and 2010 (a 40 percent drop) and to decline further thereafter. It was also decided not to restructure public debt, with the implication that the debt was supposed to be paid back gradually. This prompted many to argue that blame for the fiscal austerity program, and the consequent loss of a quarter of Greek GDP, should be assigned primarily to the decision to protect German and French banks, the holders of large amounts of Greek bonds. But let's look at things more closely.

There is no doubt that one key reason for the fall of the Greek GDP was fiscal austerity. But it should be recalled that GDP, as a result of the global crisis of 2008–09, was falling all over the world, including in countries that could afford an increase in public spending and a cut in tax rates to support the economy. Greece could not afford those adjustments because of the terrible condition of its fiscal accounts. That said, fiscal tightening by such a massive amount caused a further recessionary push, in addition to what was coming from abroad. Its extent was initially underestimated by the troika.

Could fiscal austerity policies have been avoided? Avoiding a fiscal tightening would have meant keeping the deficit at its 2009 level. Who would have financed that deficit? As European banks were no longer willing to do it, the financing would have had to come from the IMF and the European partners. But why should the European taxpayers have taken upon themselves the task of keeping unchanged Greece's standard of living, which had increased in the run-up to the crisis well beyond Greece's capacity to produce income? A fiscal tightening was therefore inevitable.

Would a more gradual fiscal adjustment have been possible had the decision been made to restructure public debt from the beginning? For example, Greece could have decided to repay only 50 percent of its debt. In that case the fiscal tightening could have been less strong, but not by much. The reason is that most of Greece's fiscal deficit originated not in interest payments but in the underlying primary deficit. In 2009 the Greek fiscal deficit exceeded 15.5 percent of GDP. The primary deficit, however, was about 10.5 percent of GDP, while interest payments on government debt were 5 percent of GDP. This means that even if public debt and interest payments had been halved, it would still have been necessary for Greece to cut spending or increase taxes by an amount equal to 12.5 percent of GDP to maintain a balanced budget after the debt restructuring, owing to the difficulty of borrowing in markets after a default. In other words, the primary cause of the deficit was not the burden of interest payments but the huge imbalance between revenues and noninterest spending.

Of course, the adjustment could have been more gradual had debt restructuring been accompanied by sizable financing from the international community, as this would have avoided the immediate need to balance the budget. But there were good reasons—at least on the side of the European partners, and to some extent also on the Greek side—to avoid or at least to postpone a debt restructuring. First, about a third of public debt was held by Greek residents. For this part a debt restructuring would have been equivalent to a tax, with recessionary effects on the economy, as discussed in the previous chapter. Of the rest, the bulk was held by European investors, primarily European banks. But behind the banks were a number of households and firms that, indirectly at least, could have suffered a loss from a haircut on Greek debt. Part of the loss would have been absorbed by bank profits, but there would have been repercussions for those who lend to banks, depositors and other savers, through lower deposit rates. Or banks could have tried to offset the losses by raising the rates at which they were lending to their customers. These effects would have been fairly modest, however, because Greek debt was small with respect to the size of the European economy.

A second, and much more significant, reason to avoid or postpone restructuring the Greek debt was contagion risk. Other European countries were concerned that a debt restructuring in Greece would have made investors afraid that the same approach would be followed for other high-debt countries—Italy, Portugal, Ireland, Spain—economies that were in aggregate some fourteen times the size of the Greek economy. Better to avoid, then, a debt restructuring, at least until a European safety net (a system of financing for countries subject to market pressure) could be set up, to reassure investors that contagion effects from a Greek debt restructuring could be avoided.

There was an intense debate within the IMF on whether the IMF should have requested a restructuring of public debt as a condition to lend to Greece. Views differed among the IMF staff, but eventually the IMF decided to go ahead without a debt restructuring. The potential for a contagion effect remained contained. In May 2010, at the beginning of the Greek program, the interest rate spread on other high-debt countries remained quite low (125 basis points for Italy, for example). We will never know what would have happened if Greece had defaulted on its debt in early 2010. What we know is that the restructuring of public debt in late 2011 was not the decisive move for the Greek economy that its supporters had hoped it would be, and was definitely accompanied by the dramatic contagion effects that shocked the whole euro area and brought Italy close to needing to request support from the IMF.

Thus, I believe that the decision not to restructure Greek public debt in 2010 was the right one. And perhaps the first financing program to support Greece could have succeeded if two big mistakes had not been made.

The Mistakes of the First Financing Program and the Second Financing Program

The first mistake was to lend to Greece at unsustainable conditions with respect to interest levels and maturities. These lending terms increased the austerity dosage that was needed and reduced the credibility of an eventual debt repayment by Greece. About three quarters of the financing to Greece was provided by European countries. The spread on this financing over the Eurobor (the rate used for short-term loans among European banks) was close to 400 basis points, plus an additional 50 basis points that Greece had to pay for each installment of the financing. This was less than what Greece would have paid if it had borrowed in the markets (assuming some entity had been willing to lend to Greece), but it was a very high interest rate. Moreover, the maturity of the financing was not long enough: repayment was slated to start within five years and be completed within eight years, not a very long time if one considers the size of the Greek public debt and the fact that deficits would have made it difficult for Greece to regain access quickly to financial markets to repay the official lenders. The financing granted by the IMF was not much cheaper, but the IMF has its own rules, and its non-European members most likely would not have agreed to a change in the interest rate on IMF loans just to accommodate the needs of a European country. However, the European loans could have been granted on much better terms. Why this was not done is a matter of speculation. Perhaps it was the desire to punish Greece for its own economic sins. In any case, such severe financing conditions required even more austerity, which contributed to the fall in GDP and reduced the credibility of the adjustment program.

The second mistake was equally serious: on the one hand, the program assumed that debt restructuring was not necessary; on the other hand, it was hinted that a restructuring might be needed at a later date. Let me explain.

The decision not to restructure Greek public debt was seen by many as a favor to those who had invested in Greece, including German and French banks. The international community, some argued, gave money to Athens to allow Greece to repay the loans it had received from French and German banks, which had greatly profited from those loans.

These arguments were not entirely valid. If the program had worked, private investors (let's call them "the banks," even if things are more complicated, as we have seen) would sooner or later have started lending again to Greece. The loans from the international community would have been repaid at that point, and so ultimately, there would have not been any bailout of investors. By the way, most of the loans to Greece had been granted by foreign banks when interest rates were quite low, at a time when financial markets were still enthusiastic regarding the creation of the euro area, so one cannot even say that the banks had enjoyed the payment of a high risk premium.

But the pressure on European governments for some form of "punishment" for the private creditors who had benefited from lending to Greece was mounting. And so, just a few months after the inception of the adjustment program, Nicolas Sarkozy and Angela Merkel, during a summit held in the French city of Deauville on October 19, 2010, announced that the private sector should contribute to the financing of countries in crisis: the term used was "private sector involvement," a euphemism for debt restructuring. Some noted that the timing of the announcement had been picked to allow French and German banks to sell their Greek bonds soon after the beginning of the program in May, but that is hearsay. In principle, the need to involve the private sector referred only to future support programs, not to Greece's program, and was coupled with the announcement of the creation of a permanent mechanism to finance European countries in crisis, the European Stability Mechanism, endowed with several hundred billion euros provided by eurozone member countries. But it was a clear signal to financial markets that debt restructuring was no longer taboo in Europe, including in Greece.

You can imagine the impact this had on financial markets and the credibility of the program. What would you have done with your Greek bonds if you had known that their restructuring was becoming more likely? The reaction of the financial markets was quick and fierce. Everybody tried to sell Greek bonds, and their yield spread over German bonds, which had declined by 300 basis points between early September and mid-October, surged back to 650–900 basis points in a matter of days. All this seemed to signal that the return of Greece to the markets by the spring of 2012 (which is what the program envisaged) was less and less likely. For all practical purposes, the first program was dead.

Both errors—lending to Greece at punitive rates, and envisaging the involvement of the private sector, or in other words, debt restructuring—were caused by the inability to realize that, once the decision to support Greece had been made, that should have been the only priority, and that trying to punish those who had sinned (Greece, for its excessive public deficits, and the investors, who had too easily lent money to Greece) was inconsistent with the success of the program. Support packages do have undesirable side effects: they reward inappropriate behaviors, such as lending too easily and borrowing irresponsibly. Economists describe these behaviors as posing a moral hazard. But one should worry about moral hazard issues once the crisis has been resolved (for example, through better monitoring of public finances and more effective financial market regulation), not in the middle of a crisis. The U.S. government learned this quite rapidly: after the refusal to support Lehman Brothers triggered the 2008–09 global financial crisis, the U.S. government intervened heavily to support the financial sector in 2009, a strategy that helped economic activity and allowed a recovery of all the money that had been used to support banks; in fact, a small profit was realized.

The increase in spreads between bond yields that followed the Deauville declaration marked the beginning of the end of the first financial support program. After a slow agony, at the end of 2011 the decision was made to restructure Greek public debt, and in the spring of 2012 a new financial support program was started. The haircut on the Greek debt was about 50 percent (equivalent to €107 billion, or more than 50 percent of 2011 GDP), a very large figure. But the public debt-to-GDP ratio declined only from 170 percent of GDP at the end of 2011 to 157 percent of GDP at the end of 2012 because of the uninterrupted decline in GDP, because the fiscal deficit remained large, and especially because of the need to support with public money the Greek banks, holders of the restructured Greek government bonds: they could not be allowed to go bankrupt, as this would have prompted a deposit run and ultimately even larger losses for bank depositors. All this shows the difficulty that debt restructuring can face in restoring the viability of public finances.

The second support program to Greece featured much lower interest rates (just a few basis points above the rate at which Germany was borrowing in the financial markets) and very long maturities (the payment of the loans is expected to be completed only by 2047). Some lenders, such as Italy, in order to lend to Greece are actually borrowing money in the financial markets at rates well above those at which money is lent to Greece through the European Stability Mechanism, which means that even if Greece repaid all its debt, some European countries would actually lose some money in the process, a concrete sign of solidarity with their euro-zone partner. But it is money well spent, as Greece's exit from the euro zone could trigger a new wave of major speculative attacks. In sum, the European lending countries have learned their lesson well, although a bit late. As a result of how events played out, the burden of interest payments is currently not very high for Greece. In 2015 the ratio between interest payments on Greek debt and GDP was just 3.6 percent, much below its level in 2007 (4.5 percent), despite the much higher debt level. As a reference, the interest payment burden for the Italian government is 4.2 percent, well above the Greek level, even though Italy has a much lower debt level.

The Greek economy started recovering during 2013, and in early 2014 a modest positive growth was finally recorded. The public deficit had declined: in May 2014 the IMF projected a deficit of about 3 percent for that year with a primary surplus of 1.5 percent. Many problems remained unresolved: for example, the fight against tax evasion had failed to yield significant results, as the heads of the Revenue Agency were repeatedly changed, often to accommodate political pressures. Many reforms remained incomplete. And productivity and competitiveness were still lagging. But in general, things were improving.

The Crisis of the Second Financing Program, and the Third Financing Program

The crisis of the second financing program was more political than economic. Granted, the anti-troika radical left had strengthened as a reaction to austerity and the fall in GDP, and it could be argued that a political crisis was inevitable as a consequence of the economic crisis. But what caused the fall of the government at the end of 2014 and the need for new elections was an accident that could easily have been avoided. The Greek parliament was dismissed and new elections were called because of parliament's inability to choose a new president of the republic, a largely honorific position in Greece. The government's candidate was lacking only ten votes. Those ten votes changed the economic history of Greece, at least for several years.

I shall not review in detail the political developments in Greece during the spring and summer of 2015, which included Alexis Tsipras's victory, the endless see-saw between anti-troika announcements and rapprochements with Europe, the referendum that rejected the new reform measures requested by Europe in exchange for a third financing program, the Greek government's about-face, and the final agreement on a new program with Europe.

What matters here is the final decision made by the Tsipras government to stay in the euro zone and continue to strengthen the fiscal accounts and structural reforms. The new adjustment program is proceeding more or less as expected. There is one major hurdle to overcome, though, in the immediate future. At the time of writing, the IMF is not yet part of the deal. The new financing is being provided entirely by the European institutions. The IMF has expressed its availability to resume its lending to Greece but requires as a condition that a major restructuring of public debt take place: most of Greece's public debt, which in the meantime has somewhat stabilized at 170 to 180 percent of GDP, is now held by European institutions and countries. The IMF wants a major restructuring of public debt because it believes that repaying public debt on current terms would require running primary surpluses so large that they would stifle economic growth over the next decades. Perhaps to underscore the importance it was giving to this issue, the IMF in 2015 took the unprecedented step of publishing its evaluation of public debt sustainability (the Debt Sustainability Assessment, or DSA) outside its normal publication cycle (usually linked to the publication of a full report on a country's economy). A first DSA was published just a few days ahead of the mid-2015 referendum when the Greek population was asked to accept or reject the conditions requested by the European institutions to resume lending. Some took it as a signal that the IMF wanted to influence the outcome of the referendum. A new DSA was published just a couple of weeks later—another unusual event—and took the view that, because of developments following the referendum, public debt had become "highly unsustainable," an expression that, to the best of my knowledge, had never before been used in a published DSA.

The IMF indicated that either a major haircut on the principal of the loans granted by Europe or, alternatively, a massive increase in the maturity of public debt (with no payments starting before 2035 and the last repayment scheduled for 2075) was absolutely needed. The Europeans have agreed to some additional debt relief measures but not of the magnitude requested by the IMF. To complicate matters, however, some European countries, including Germany, have requested that sooner or later the IMF come on board, as a European-only program would not be credible to them. And yet Germany is among the countries that most forcefully oppose a major debt relief operation. It's not an easy situation to solve.

My view is that assessing whether Greece will be able to repay its debt over the next decades—that is, assessing whether its debt is sustainable—is almost impossible at present. It all depends on how fast Greece is able to grow over the next decades while remaining in the euro zone and regaining the competitiveness it lost since its euro-zone entry. The IMF strongly believes Greece is condemned to a low-growth path unless debt is rescheduled. Of course, from the point of view of Greece, it would be better to have a lower debt. But whether it is absolutely necessary that debt be restructured—and whether this would make a difference with respect to other impediments to growth—is impossible to evaluate. It would make sense to wait for things to clarify before a major rescheduling is deemed necessary.

One last consideration: Greece is financed by the European safety net set up in 2011 to support countries in crisis. It would be a major failure for European institutions if such a safety net showed that countries that use it cannot repay their debt. What would happen the next time a country was hit by a crisis? Would the safety net still be available?

The bottom line is that an agreement still needs to be found. We shall see how all this ends.

Lessons of the Greek Crisis

There are four lessons to be drawn from the Greek crisis.

First, there are periods in which it is easy to sustain large fiscal deficits because investors sometimes get carried away and lend at low rates even when it would be prudent not to do it. Those periods may sometimes be quite prolonged, but they end sooner or later.

Second, in periods of economic growth, it is wise to reduce the public debt-to-GDP ratio because those periods will not last forever, and when the economy weakens public debt will tend to rise. If public debt and deficits are already high, when the economy weakens a country can easily get into trouble. Investors can rapidly change their minds, and when they do they often overreact, making it even harder for a country to get out of trouble.

Third, in the Greek case, it would have been better to lend to Greece at much more favorable conditions from the beginning, and, correspondingly, to ask for a more gradual fiscal adjustment. But it would not have been possible to avoid a significant degree of austerity in a country that was living well above its means.

Fourth, restructuring public debt is difficult even when a sizable part of it is held abroad, at least when the "abroad" is pretty close to your borders. In the Greek case the major haircut applied to public debt held by the private sector in 2012 was not the decisive move that some expected it to be, and after the debt restructuring, debt resumed its growth. The contagion effects of the restructuring were large. Thus the burden of proof of showing that an earlier restructuring would have been preferable falls on those who supported it. Such a proof has not yet been provided.

TWELVE

Debt Mutualization

I get by with a little help from my friends.

—*The Beatles*

Economic conditions in Europe in 2011–12 were paradoxical: some euro-zone members were suffering heavily from the first crisis faced by the euro area since its inception while others were greatly benefiting from it. Money was flowing from countries under financial market pressure (the southern European countries plus Ireland), pushing interest rates up, to those of northern Europe (especially Germany), pushing interest rates down. The money flow was caused by the fear that countries with low competitiveness and high debt would have to leave the euro zone. But wasn't the euro born out of an ideal vision of European economic and, in perspective, political unity? And did this ideal goal not imply some degree of solidarity among European countries? If so, why should stronger countries that were actually benefiting from the crisis not support the countries that were suffering from speculative attacks? After all, as the Beatles said, we get by with a little help from our friends.

Perhaps as a reflection of this general feeling that solidarity was needed among European countries, many different proposals were put forward on how euro-zone countries could "share risk." This chapter discusses these risk-sharing proposals, including those specifically relating to the fiscal accounts (there were also risk-sharing proposals relating to the financial sector, such as the introduction of a common deposit insurance). Among these proposals we will look more closely at those that essentially implied "mutualizing" public debt, that is, replacing debt issued by individual countries with debt issued by a European institution, perhaps a European ministry of finance, thus reducing the risk of crisis for high-debt countries.

While the focus of this chapter is on euro-zone countries, we will also talk about the experience of other areas of the world, especially the experience of federal states. Indeed, the main lesson of this chapter is that debt mutualization requires a kind of solidarity that is not found even in those common currency areas that have reached a full degree of political unity, such as federal states (the United States, Canada). It is therefore unrealistic to expect that mutualization will occur on a large scale in the euro zone, which is still far from political unity.

Sharing Risks in a Monetary Union

Many economists have argued that the good working of a monetary union—an economic area sharing the same currency—requires some degree of risk sharing: if a member of the area is hit by a shock specific to that member (economists call them "idiosyncratic" or "asymmetric" shocks) or a shock to the whole area that affects members to a different degree, that member should be helped by other members of the union. Risk sharing is needed because when countries become members of a currency union, they lose one key tool to absorb economic shocks: they no longer have an independent monetary and exchange rate policy. Moreover, their fiscal policy also typically becomes subject to common fiscal rules. Helping countries hit by a shock is in everybody's interest because a crisis in a currency union member can easily spill over to the rest of the union. Thus at least those members that respect the rules of the monetary club should benefit from the support of other club members.

That is the theory. In practice, risk sharing is much less common and less extensive than many believe, especially when it comes to public debt, even in common currency areas that have reached a full political union, such as federal states.[1]

Other currency union members can help members hit by an economic shock in three ways. The first one is to transfer to them unrequited resources. The second one is to lend them money that will need to be paid back in due course. The third one is to mutualize debt, either by issuing common debt or by guaranteeing the debt issued by the country hit by the shock.

Let's start with transferring money without asking for anything in exchange. This issue has been studied considerably by economists since the euro zone came into being. Indeed, as soon as the project of a common currency area was announced in the early 1990s, many economists noted that in the existing common currency areas, such as the United States, members hit by a recession receive sizable net transfers from the central government. In other words, the difference between the resources received from the central budget and those transferred to the central budget increased when a member country (state, province) was in trouble. Should this not also be done in the euro area? Many proposals for achieving this sort of arrangement have been put forward over time, including by the European Commission and the International Monetary Fund (IMF).[2]

Most such studies, however, do not take into account one important feature of the net transfers that take place in federal states: they occur as a by-product of the centralization in the federal budget of certain tax and spending policies.[3] The bulk of the increase in net transfers during a recession comes from the centralization of income taxes: the residents of the currency member pay lower taxes to the federal budget when they are hit by a recession. Moreover, if there is a central unemployment insurance system, the residents of the member in crisis receive larger transfers from the center. By contrast, ad hoc transfers aimed specifically to dampen the effect of shocks hitting individual member countries are quite uncommon. There are exceptions, as in the case of the transfers made in 2009 in the United States from the federal budget to the states in response to the global crisis, but such cases are certainly not the rule. This is not a minor distinction: an increase in net transfers arising from centralized policies—which is entirely automatic and a by-product of a much broader decision to have a sizable federal budget—is probably less politically sensitive than ad hoc transfers to offset shocks, particularly if the shocks affect only a discrete group of countries, whose troubles may appear to be self-inflicted or at least facilitated by irresponsible behavior on the part of the countries in crisis. That is perhaps why ad hoc transfers are less common.

Unfortunately, the mechanism of net transfers through a federal budget would not work in Europe, where taxing and spending policies are almost entirely decentralized and where the European Union (EU) budget is tiny, being more or less one-twentieth the size of the federal budgets of even the most decentralized federal states. Some member countries, such as Italy, have put forward proposals to centralize some fiscal policies, for example unemployment benefit policies, but such a centralization clashes with the still dominant wish not too give up too much sovereignty.[4] Altogether, we should not be too surprised by the lack of progress in setting up ad hoc transfer mechanisms, as these are not common even in federal states.

The second way to share risk is to lend money to countries hit by a shock. The loans should be granted with affordable conditions, which was not the case in the first financing program to Greece. But in the euro zone there is now a better framework to lend to countries in crisis at rates that do not jeopardize from the outset the chances of repayment. In this respect, there has indeed been progress in the euro zone. This follows the experience of at least some federal states. Indeed, whereas in the United States the federal budget has never stepped in to support states in financial trouble (since 1840), in other federal states lending to subnational governments is not uncommon when they find themselves in trouble, as in the case of support provided in Germany in the past to its *Lander* (the German term for "regions" or "states").

In the previous chapter we described the European Stability Mechanism (ESM), the institution that, in the absence of a sizable central budget, has been set up in Europe with the specific goal of lending to euro-zone countries in crisis. The ESM is currently headed by Klaus Regling, a former IMF staff and EU Commission member, an excellent economist and an expert in European institutions. The ESM lends to member countries in exchange for fiscal and structural adjustment policies, as is done by the IMF. The procedures that need to be followed for the disbursements of the loan tranches are quite complex, but complexity is the norm when it comes to EU procedures and rules. The most important thing to be kept in mind in the context of this chapter is that the solidarity arising from the ESM loans relates to countries that have already been hit by a crisis. These loans cannot be used by high-debt countries to lower their exposure to financial markets and in this way reduce the risk of a crisis. In other words, they are not a useful solution to the problems arising from high public debt discussed in this book.

European Debt to Replace Individual Countries' Debt

The third approach to risk sharing in a monetary union is the one that interests us more closely: it is the possibility of pulling together each country's public debt, or part of it, and replacing it with debt issued or guaranteed by the center, by a European institution set up for this purpose or already existing, such as the European Commission or the European Investment Bank, so as to reduce the risk of a crisis in high-debt countries.

There have been many proposals to mutualize public debt in the euro zone, but most are based on the same basic idea. A European institution borrows from financial markets by issuing bonds that are guaranteed by all euro-zone members: the magic legal words are that the guarantee is "joint and several," which means that each euro-zone member could be asked to pay, if there are problems, the whole amount of the maturing bond of the country in trouble.[5] With the "joint and several" guarantee in place, the bonds are issued at low interest rates and the resources are used to buy bonds issued by individual countries at higher interest rates. This strategy would remove from the markets a sizable amount of high interest rate bonds, amounting in some proposals to up to 60 percent of GDP. The member countries therefore would become debtors to the European institution and no longer to the capricious financial markets, and would repay their debt over time, perhaps benefiting from a somewhat lower interest rate in exchange for the provision of real guarantees, for example, the real estate they own.[6]

The financial schemes proposed are often very smart in their technical details, but they have not progressed at all in terms of implementation. The underlying reason for this lack of progress is that these schemes require a degree of solidarity—a degree of altruism—that is unheard of even in federal states, that is, in the common currency areas that have abandoned many aspects of their sovereignty and are part of a single nation. Of course, federal states do issue federal debt, but to finance federal deficits, not the deficit of single member countries, nor to replace the debt originally issued by single members of the federation.[7]

In federal states each member (each U.S. state, each German Land) is responsible for financing its own deficit and debt. It is a matter of principle, needed to avoid free-riding behavior, that is, dumping on other member countries the cost of one's own profligacy. There have been exceptions to this approach in economic history, but under very special circumstances.

When the United States emerged after the war of independence, the debt of the single states was replaced by federal debt. But that debt had originated in a war fought in common against the British and not from, say, welfare spending or, worse, purely wasteful public spending by individual states.[8] Another specific case of replacement of the debt of individual states by the debt of the new nation arising from their merger is represented by Italy. When in 1861 a unitary state was formed, the debt of individual states was replaced by a national debt. The reason for this, however, was not solidarity but selfishness on the part of the state (the Regno di Sardegna, which, despite its name, was centered in Piedmont, a northern Italian region), which was leading Italy's unification and had a public debt much higher than the combined debt of the states that were going to be absorbed.[9]

Why, then, should euro-zone lower-debt countries take on the burden of higher public debt euro-zone countries? Of course, many good reasons can be adduced, including that the good functioning of the euro area requires it and thus everybody would eventually benefit from it. But again, in practice this is not what happens in other currency areas, not even in federal states.

A Postscript on "PADRE"

To conclude this chapter, I will mention one of the few proposals that have been put forward to lower public debt in Europe that do not require a guarantee by all member countries and so does not require the kind of altruism that appears unreasonable to expect, based on historical experience.

The proposal, titled "Politically Acceptable Debt Restructuring in Europe," whose acronym, PADRE, means "father" in Italian, comes from two French economists, Pierre Pâris and Charles Wyplosz.[10] Its basic idea is brilliant. Each euro-zone member owns an asset whose value is fairly safe, but because the member state does not control the asset directly, it can be credibly used as collateral or sold, even if it produces an income stream only over time. This asset is given by the net present value (the discounted sum) of its share of future profits of the European Central Bank (ECB). These profits depend on the capacity of the ECB to print banknotes whose intrinsic value and production cost are very low but which are accepted in exchange for goods and services (this capacity is what in chapter 1 we identified as *seigniorage*, the right to print money). The amount of these profits over the next few decades, the two economists argue, is fairly certain, unless a dramatic change in the use of banknotes occurs (which is possible, but the authors assume it is not).

The European countries could give up the right to receive these profits and in this way could endow with capital an institution that had the task of absorbing, at zero interest rate, half of the euro-zone bonds in circulation. The result would be a halving of the value of public debt present in financial markets. The purchases of government bonds across countries by this institution, which could be the ECB, would be proportional to each country's share in the capital of the ECB, and hence proportional to its share of ECB profits. There would be no need for a guarantee by any of the member states because the source of profits would be the ECB itself, and thus there would be no way for a country to renege on its promise. That is the nice thing about this proposal. In principle, the same approach could be followed for any other future government income stream. The government could sell, for example, its future personal income tax stream, but could later change its mind (as sovereign countries do sometimes). This would not be possible for the seigniorage income stream, which is controlled by the ECB. Initially the scheme would run at a loss because the ECB profits would not be enough to cover the losses on the purchased bonds, but what matters is that the discounted value of the seigniorage income stream would be large enough to cover the discounted value of losses on the bond conversion.

The PADRE proposal has two problems, though. The first is that any country's giving up its share of ECB profits would weaken its fiscal revenues for the future. Debt would indeed decline, but so would the future value of revenues. The second problem is an empirical one: it is not at all clear whether the value of seigniorage is sufficient to cover the cost of the operation, especially if one considers possible changes in payment technologies in the future: in a credit-card-only world, the use of banknotes and seigniorage could collapse.

In any case, even the PADRE proposal has not made any progress. I believe that, pragmatically, it is better to think about reducing euro-zone public debt without relying on its mutualization or other financial engineering operations.

THIRTEEN

Privatization

In theory there is no difference between theory and practice: in practice there is.

—*Yogi Berra, attributed*

I n many countries, public debt is managed by a department of the Ministry of Finance (or sometimes by a separate agency or separate ministry) called the Treasury. The name reveals that once the key task of this part of the public administration was to manage not so much public debt as the real and financial assets of the sovereign, the crown's treasury. In a historical perspective, public debt is a relatively recent invention, as described by Niall Ferguson in chapter 4 of *The Cash Nexus*, unlike private debt, which dates back thousands of years.[1] But before public debt ever existed, there was a need to manage the sovereign's wealth—the crown's jewels, so to speak—and the one who was responsible for this was the king's treasurer.

When a government is short of cash, it is obvious to wonder whether it would not be possible to sell the government's assets—the crown's jewels, accumulated in good times or simply inherited from the distant past—rather than tax people. That is exactly what the Roman emperor Marcus Aurelius did in A.D. 167 to finance the Marcomannic Wars: according to Eutropius, the sale lasted two months in the Trajan Forum and was quite successful. It would be followed by many other sales, or "privatizations," as we would call them now. Indeed, whenever a country is hit by a crisis, as in the case of Greece or, on a smaller scale, of Italy in 2011–12, you can be almost certain that someone will try to pull the privatization rabbit out of the hat. Privatization is often seen as a painless solution to high public debt. In parallel, ambitious plans are often drafted on how to increase the yield on government assets so as to finance the payment of interest on public debt.

Unfortunately, bridging the gap between privatization plans and privatization reality is often quite difficult; hence the epigraph at the opening of this chapter.[2]

How Large Are Government Assets?

Very few countries publish or even keep a comprehensive balance sheet, one that includes not only assets but also liabilities. The United Kingdom produces the Whole of Government Accounts, which includes a consolidated balance sheet of the U.K. public sector,[3] and the United States publishes with some lag a financial report that includes a balance sheet, but only for the federal government. Most countries do not publish a full balance sheet. They do publish various kinds of information about the assets owned by the public sector, but the criteria used for asset valuation are different across countries and often do not reflect market values.

That said, the Organization for Economic Cooperation and Development (OECD) does publish cross-country information on the value of the financial and nonfinancial assets of its members, and at first sight the figures are quite impressive. In advanced economies the government financial wealth might exceed 40 percent of GDP, while nonfinancial wealth (buildings, structures, land, and so on) in the OECD countries might average 65 to 70 percent of GDP. Altogether, we are talking about total government assets averaging some 100 percent of GDP, an impressive figure. Of course, there are large differences across countries, with some countries, such as Switzerland, showing nonfinancial assets of less than 20 percent of GDP and others, such as Korea, showing figures well above 100 percent of GDP. Moreover, what matters for us is not the average but the assets of high-debt countries. But the figures are quite impressive even for some high-debt countries. For example, according to the OECD, just the nonfinancial assets of the Italian public sector would amount to 80 percent of GDP and those of France would amount to some 100 percent of GDP. Why not sell at least part of those assets to bring down public debt?

The Case for Selling Government Assets

We should ask first whether it would make sense to sell public assets to repay public liabilities. A common objection is that selling government assets to repay liabilities does not change the government's net worth. Liabilities go down, assets go down; the net does not change. So why bother? Leaving aside more general considerations (including the belief on the part of some that raising the share of assets managed by the private sector improves the efficiency of the economic system and hence growth), there are at least two good reasons why high public debt countries should sell their public assets.

The first reason has to do with the low liquidity of public sector assets. High public debt implies that the government's gross borrowing requirement (how much the government needs to borrow to repay maturing debt and to finance any deficit) can be very large. This constant need for new liquid resources exposes the government to the risk of a crisis, a risk that is not much reduced by the existence of government assets. The assets of the government may be large, but selling them during a liquidity crisis is virtually impossible, sometimes even at fire sale prices (analogous to the difficulty of selling quickly government-owned real estate). These assets can perhaps be sold in good times and gradually but not quickly during a liquidity crisis. To reduce the risk of a crisis, therefore, it is better to sell them gradually and use the proceeds to repay public debt.

The second reason why selling assets to repay debt may be a good idea has to do with the yield of the government assets. The yield is often quite low, even when the interest rate on government bonds is high. For example, the average yield of Italian public sector assets has been estimated to have been 0.5 to 1 percent in 2011–12, when the government was borrowing at rates of 5 to 6 percent. Therefore, selling low-yield government assets to repay high-cost public debt involves a net saving. An alternative would be to try to raise the yield of government assets, and this is something that should definitely be done (even if one believes that, in a market economy, it is not necessarily better to let the government manage assets when these could probably more efficiently be managed by the private sector; of course, there are many cases in which public ownership is necessary, but public ownership should remain limited to cases of market failure). But in practice, neither selling government assets nor increasing their yield is as easy as supporters of this route to solve the public debt problem seem to believe.

Why It Is Difficult to Sell Government Assets, or to Raise Their Yield

There are at least three reasons why it is difficult to increase government revenues by selling government assets or increasing their yield.

First, there are vested interests in the status quo. Selling public assets means taking away power from those who are currently administering those assets. Moreover, increasing the yield of public assets means asking those who are using them—private sector households and firms—to pay more for using them. There are bound to be objections. Nonetheless, I do not think this is the key obstacle, at least relative to other solutions to high public debt, as powerful vested interests would also have to be overcome to implement orthodox fiscal adjustments.

Second, not much that is owned by the public sector has a very high market value in practice. The official data I gave earlier in the chapter are in this respect quite misleading, for a number of reasons:

- Among financial assets, some governments still own shares in companies whose shares are traded on stock exchanges. This is probably the component of public sector assets that can most easily be sold, but the amounts are no longer as high as they were, for example, in the 1960s, as a lot has already been sold.

- Other financial assets, whose value inflates the official statistics, cannot be sold at all, or at least not easily. These assets often include credits to the private sector arising from unpaid taxes. The financial assets of euro-zone countries currently include large amounts of direct loans to Greece or their share in the European Stability Mechanism, which obviously cannot be sold. They also include euro-zone countries' share in the capital of international financial institutions such as the International Monetary Fund (IMF), which also cannot be sold. Finally, the reported financial assets of the central government sometimes include credits to the rest of the public administration, which would be pointless to sell.

- When it comes to real assets, the bulk is represented by buildings and, to a lesser extent, land. Many buildings, however, cannot easily be sold as they are used by the public administration. Then there are buildings with historical and artistic value: could the French government possibly sell the Eiffel Tower? Other properties, such as unused army barracks, could be sold but would require upfront investment costs.

The third reason why increasing revenues through privatization can be difficult has to do with the complexity of the operation. In most countries, public sector assets are owned not by the central government but by thousands of local governments, some of which may not have any debt at all, so the sale of these assets could not be used to repay public debt, short of the expropriation of local properties by the central government. Even for the central government, coordinating the sale of properties owned or controlled by different ministries would not be as easy as it might appear in theory. Moreover, the public sector would need adequate human skills to manage the asset sale, and those skills can be missing in some countries. Finally, market conditions may not be right for selling and may be worsened by the news that the government is selling, for example, large shares of its real estate properties.

In sum, there is no reason why the sale of public sector assets should not contribute to the reduction of public debt in high-debt countries, but one must be realistic about the amount of revenues that can come from privatizing government assets or from attempting to raise their yield. The risk is that medium-term debt reduction plans based on large privatization revenues are simply not credible, given the existing obstacles. And, more generally, what can reasonably be sold often is much less than what the official figures show. Italy is a case in point. Public debt is now some 133 percent of GDP. Some economists estimated a few years ago that, with a major investment of political capital, it would be possible to raise revenues from government assets amounting to 15 percent of GDP over a ten-year period, or 1.5 percent of GDP per year. This is definitely an ambitious target, as privatization revenues in Italy have averaged around 0.2 to 0.3 percent of GDP over the last four years. But even quintupling the amount of privatization revenues per year over the next ten years would allow a reduction in the public debt ratio by only fifteen percentage points of GDP, just a fraction of the 133 percent of GDP debt stock. Privatization should continue, in my view, not least because the public sector in Italy has a presence in areas where there is no clear market failure and where the private sector could probably be more effective. But privatization by itself does not represent the ultimate solution to the problem of high public debt, in Italy or in other countries.

My work at the IMF over the past three decades has taught me the need to be very prudent when it comes to estimating privatization revenues. Because higher privatization revenues are viewed as an alternative to making more painful cuts, their announcement is generally taken positively, and governments with a high-debt crisis tend to overestimate their amounts and to underestimate related implementation difficulties. One persistent problem of Greek adjustment programs over the last few years has been the overestimation of privatization receipts. Repeated failure to achieve the privatization targets has certainly damaged the overall credibility of Greece's economic adjustment strategy.

A Postscript on Public Debt Management

I started this chapter by saying that in earlier centuries, the main responsibility of the government treasurer was to manage government wealth. That is no longer the case. The main responsibility of the Treasury is now to manage public debt, essentially deciding what kinds of securities to issue, how to sell them, and to what extent to hedge the related interest rate and currency risks. Sometimes governments hope to be able to save considerable amounts of money through more skilled debt management. My experience is that public debt managers in advanced economies are already pretty good at their job, and there is not much room for improvement. Of course, the cost of borrowing can be lowered by assuming more risk, or vice versa. But free lunches are rare. It's better not to look for dangerous shortcuts.

Part III

THE MAIN ROAD

FOURTEEN

Economic Growth

Grow your way out of debt? Don't make us laugh.

—*Bill Bonner*

This chapter is about the "motherhood and apple pie" solution to the high public debt conundrum. Who could be against motherhood and apple pie? And who could be against growing one's way out of high public debt? This chapter considers how effective an increase in growth could be in lowering the public debt-to-GDP ratio. But the chapter also has two additional, and less reassuring, points to make. First, it is not so easy to raise the long-term growth of the economy, and that is really what matters in lowering, at a steady pace, the public debt ratio, not the economy's short-term growth rate. Second, a higher long-term growth rate is much more effective in lowering the public debt ratio if the revenues from higher growth do not lead to additional spending and are instead saved (at least to some extent). So some degree of fiscal austerity is also needed. Thus the chapter is also a bridge to the following chapter, which discusses the role of moderate fiscal austerity in lowering public debt ratios in advanced economies.

The Power of Growth

The potentially huge impact of an increase in the long-term growth rate of the economy on the public debt-to-GDP ratio is easily illustrated with an example. Let's consider a country that starts with a public debt-to-GDP ratio of 130 percent and a level of taxation of 43 percent. That means that when GDP goes up by 100 dollars, the government's tax revenues go up by 43 dollars. It is a large figure, but not too different from the tax ratio of several high-debt countries, at least in Europe.[1] For the United Kingdom, Japan, and the United States, the ratios would be lower (respectively 34, 28, and 27 percent), so the numbers reported below exaggerate the effect of the impact of growth on public debt, but the mechanisms at work are the same.

Let's also assume for simplicity that initially the fiscal deficit and the GDP growth rate are such as to keep the public debt ratio constant at 130 percent. This would require, for example, a deficit of 3.8 percent of GDP and a growth rate of nominal GDP of 3 percent (say, 2 percent inflation plus 1 percent real growth).[2] This is our baseline scenario.

What happens if the economy's growth rate increases from 1 to 2 percent, that is, by one percentage point in real terms, so that the nominal growth rate rises from 3 percent per year to 4 percent per year? Let's first assume that all tax revenues from higher growth are saved. In this case—you can check this with a simple Excel spreadsheet—the public debt-to-GDP ratio will decline to 101 percent after ten years and to 72 percent after fifteen years, an almost sixty percentage point drop from the initial level. This would be great. Have we found the solution to the high public debt problem? Let's see. This huge decline in the debt ratio occurs for two reasons. The first is simply that GDP, the denominator of the ratio, increases faster than in the baseline (stable) scenario, so the ratio declines; the second is that faster GDP growth means a faster increase in tax revenues and hence a lower deficit, as revenues are saved by assumption. Of these two forces the second is by far the more powerful, particularly in countries with higher tax ratios. Indeed, if we repeat the experiment under the assumption that all revenues from higher growth are not saved but spent, then we find that, purely as a result of the increase in the denominator of the ratio (GDP), the debt ratio still declines, but by much less: after ten years the debt ratio would have declined to 119 percent and after fifteen years it would have declined to 114 percent, only sixteen percentage points below the baseline.

All this is telling us two things: first, that raising a country's long-term growth rate can really make a difference in lowering public debt; and second, that most of the effect materializes if the additional revenues, or at least part of them, are saved, something that the supporters of growth as the silver bullet to reduce the public debt ratio need to keep in mind. Of course, the temptation to spend more when growth and revenues accelerate is strong. And it would be unrealistic to expect that all additional revenues from faster growth are saved. Indeed, in the above example in which all additional revenues are saved, the government deficit, close to 4 percent in the baseline scenario, would turn into a 3.5 percent of GDP surplus after fifteen years, something that would certainly be difficult to sustain politically even in a high-debt country. So, part of the additional revenues is bound to be spent. But the point I want to make is that an effort should be made to save at least part of the additional revenues from higher growth to push the primary surplus to a higher level and lower the deficit by a sizable amount.

All this explains something that we have observed in economic history, namely, that periods of fast reductions in the public debt ratio may be characterized by sustained growth but usually also feature a strong strengthening of the primary balance, which is a key driving force in lowering the debt ratio. According to the IMF historical public debt database, the United Kingdom at the end of the Napoleonic Wars had a public debt ratio as high as 226 percent of GDP.[3] It managed to lower it during the following century to 27 percent of GDP, just before World War I. GDP growth was sustained during that period, but the additional revenues were partly saved. Niall Ferguson, the Harvard historian and author of *The Cash Nexus*, notes that between 1816 and 1899 the government deficit exceeded 1 percent of GDP in only four years, while the primary surplus averaged 4.6 percent of GDP, with peaks of 10 to 11 percent of GDP in some years.[4] The United Kingdom also experienced a period of sustained decline in the public debt ratio after World War II, when the government budget presented surpluses from 1948 to 1972, with a reduction in the public debt from 240 percent to 62 percent of GDP.

Saving the revenues arising from economic growth does require some fiscal discipline, some degree of fiscal austerity, and that is the centerpiece of the moderate fiscal austerity strategy advocated in the next chapter. But first we must take up a most challenging problem: how can we raise GDP growth?

Pulling Oneself Up by One's Bootstraps

Let's first discuss a tempting approach. As discussed in chapter 4, growth is positively affected by an increase in the fiscal deficit, at least in the short run: if the government spends more, or if it cuts taxes, aggregate demand increases (other things being the same) and, if there is spare capacity in the economy (remember the example of the car factory whose production depends on demand), GDP increases. Would it be possible, then, to boost GDP growth by a fiscal expansion that would turn out to have a beneficial effect on the public debt ratio? That would indeed be nice. It would be very much like pulling oneself up by one's bootstraps, and so, instinctively, it does not sound right. But under certain circumstances it may actually be true, at least for a while, as has recently been argued by a number of economists and, perhaps surprisingly, by the International Monetary Fund (IMF).

Let's take it step by step. The plain vanilla version of this pseudo-Keynesian solution to the high debt problem (though I really do not think that Keynes would have subscribed to it; see chapter 4) immediately faces some arithmetic difficulties, and I would not even mention it were it not for the fact that many politicians seem to buy it. Let's take a country that has a public debt of $1,300, a GDP of $1,000 (so the debt ratio is 130 percent), and, for simplicity, a balanced budget (no increase in debt in dollars) and no growth (no increase in nominal GDP), so that the debt ratio remains constant over time. Let's increase public spending by $20. What effect does this increase have on GDP and on the debt ratio? More spending by the government means more demand: we assume that demand and GDP (there is spare capacity in the economy, so GDP is determined by the demand side) go up by the same amount as government spending. In other words, we assume that the fiscal multiplier is 1 (the *fiscal multiplier* is the ratio between the increase in government spending, or a reduction in tax revenues, and the related increase in GDP).[5] In this case GDP rises to $1,020. Let's also assume that the average level of taxation is 40 percent (this is a European country with fairly high taxation). In this case, when GDP goes up by $20, revenues go up by $8 ($20×0.4). The deficit therefore increases from zero (the budget was balanced) to $12 (spending goes up by $20, but revenues go up by $8). The deterioration is not as strong as the initial spending increase, but still, the deficit increases.

What happens to the public debt ratio? The government will need to borrow another $12 to finance its new deficit, so debt will rise to $1,312. However, the ratio between public debt and GDP will now be 128.6 percent ($1,312 ÷ $1,020). So the public debt ratio declines as a result of an increase in public spending!

However, let's not get carried away, and see what happens the following year. The deficit remains at $12, so debt increases by another $12, to $1,324. As the level of government spending does not change further, the level of GDP also does not change further, so GDP stays at $1,020. Here is the key point: it is important to distinguish between GDP level and GDP growth. An increase in public spending raises the GDP level in the year when it occurs and in the following years, but the GDP growth rate increases only in the first year and then goes back to zero, while the deficit increases permanently. The debt-to-GDP ratio is now 129.8 percent, higher than the previous year. The following year, because of the same mechanism, the debt ratio will rise to 131.0 percent, and it will continue to increase thereafter.[6] Note finally that as time goes by, and in particular as the economy gets close to full employment, the increased spending by the government will be offset by less spending by the private sector because more of the limited saving available at full employment will be absorbed by the public sector (the crowding-out effect discussed in chapter 4). In other words, the fiscal multiplier declines over time and the debt ratio increases further.

When these observations are taken together, it is not possible for a government to solve the problem by pulling itself up by its fiscal bootstraps, except in some specific cases that the supporters of this view—most recently some prominent U.S. economists, as well as the IMF—are arguing are prevailing now. To be honest, the argument has been put forward (except in its more extreme versions, mentioned below) primarily to argue that a fiscal expansion can be used to support economic activity without endangering the fiscal accounts, not really to argue that a fiscal expansion should be the centerpiece of a strategy to achieve a steady decline in the public debt ratio. However, the argument, if taken literally, also implies that an increase in spending, especially public investment (though some use the same argument to call for tax cuts), does lower the public debt-to-GDP ratio in the short and long run. Let's see how this would work and the limits of this approach. There are basically two variants.

The first variant has been put forward by some influential American economists, among them former Treasury secretary Larry Summers and Nobel laureate Paul Krugman. Their basic idea is that, starting from a situation of unemployment, a temporary increase in public spending could lead not only to a short-term increase in demand and GDP but to a permanent increase in the level of potential output in comparison to a situation in which unemployment is left to fester and the unemployed lose their human capital, becoming unable to reenter the labor market. In such a case, good public investment, which would also raise the economy's potential output because long-term growth requires good infrastructure, could be self-financing, or more than self-financing, as it would bring in more revenues on a permanent basis and hence could lead to a decline in the public debt ratio.[7] Paradoxically, this view is reminiscent of Reaganomics, which promised that a permanent tax cut, undertaken without offsetting spending cuts, would boost potential output levels, and perhaps even potential growth, so much that deficits and debt would decline in the long run. However, during Reagan's presidency, public debt increased by some twenty percentage points of GDP (see chapter 5). Nevertheless, this more extreme version of pulling oneself up by one's bootstraps is now a centerpiece of the emerging fiscal strategy of President Trump, at least based on his campaign rhetoric.

The second variant has been put forward by the IMF in a recent paper written by top officials of that institution. The paper reads, "Under certain conditions . . . fiscal stimulus can improve the debt ratio (relative to a scenario with no policy response following a contractionary shock) in the long term, and even in the near term."[8] The argument made by the IMF hinges on relatively high levels of the fiscal multipliers for public investment, on the assumption that the additional spending would be financed by printing money and on the hypothesis that inflation would increase as a result of the fiscal stimulus. All of this would raise the level of nominal GDP, thus lowering the debt-to-GDP ratio more than in the scenarios I presented earlier in this section, which described just the response of real GDP, without any impact on inflation.

In all these cases, the possibility of lowering the public debt ratio through a fiscal expansion hinges critically on two assumptions, in addition to those already listed.

The first assumption is that interest rates on public debt remain low when public spending goes up. This is unlikely to be the case for high public debt countries in Europe, countries that do not have their own central bank and that have been subject in the past to sizable speculative attacks affecting their interest rate spread against German bonds. As for other countries, such as the United States, one can instead expect that interest rates would not react much to the announcement of increased spending, especially if their central banks were willing to continue monetizing public deficits and to accept a drop in real interest rates even with a recovery of economic activity. This situation can be sustained for a while but not for too long, unless central banks accept rising and potentially accelerating inflation. So these approaches could at best lead to a fairly small reduction in the debt ratio, not to a longlasting decline, which can happen only through a stable increase in the growth rate of the economy.

The second assumption is that revenues from higher growth are actually saved and that spending can credibly be increased only temporarily, rather than lead to longer-lasting increases that would be difficult to reverse. This is a critical point as well in avoiding an increase in interest rates, and particularly the IMF paper underscores the importance of having a credible medium-term adjustment plan for those countries that start from a high level of public debt. Unfortunately, this is more easily said than done. In the first place, it is hard to be credible in promising future spending cuts when you start by increasing spending. Second, this game has already been played a few times. As head of the IMF's Fiscal Affairs Department I was among those who in 2008–09 called for exactly this kind of policy: more spending now against a plan for reducing spending tomorrow. This was necessary because of the extreme situation in which the world economy was at that time: the priority was to support demand while accepting an increase in the public debt ratio, which would be reduced over the longer term. But one cannot keep playing the same game, particularly when economic conditions are not as dire as they were in 2008–09. We are not even in a recession; we just would like a bit more growth. Moreover, public debt is now much higher. More generally, the experience with fiscal policy over the last few decades is that it has been much easier to increase fiscal deficits than to reduce them, as evidenced by the trend toward increasing public debt ratios in most advanced economies since the mid-1970s. This is a major difference between monetary policy and fiscal policy. Monetary policy expansions can more easily be reversed, in part because monetary policy decisions have been delegated to technocratic central banks. In contrast, fiscal policy is inherently more political and subject to the risk of becoming hostage to electoral cycles.

In sum, neither increased public spending nor cutting taxes seems the right way to put the public debt-to-GDP ratio on a steadily downward path, as common sense would suggest. What is needed is a permanent increase in the growth rate of the economy. It is a matter not just of bringing actual output close to potential output. What is critical is to raise the potential output growth of the economy. For this you need structural reforms.

The Myth of Structural Reforms

What do we mean by structural reforms? Let's go back to the example of the car factory. The factory currently does not produce as many cars as it could because there is not enough demand for cars. This is the current situation of some advanced economies: GDP is below its potential. By how much? The IMF estimates the so-called output gap to be about 1 percent on average for advanced economies. That means that our car factory, instead of producing the 1,000 cars it could produce, is producing only 990. If the output gap were closed, GDP would be higher and government revenues would be higher, while the fiscal deficit would be lower. But not by much. And once the output gap is closed (once our car factory reaches its production potential of 1,000 cars), for GDP and government revenues to continue rising, it is necessary to boost potential output, to expand the production capacity of the factory or, in the real world, of the economy. But how can this be done?

Potential output depends basically on three things:

- First, how much firms invest in plants at home. If car sales rise to 1,000, then our car firm may decide to invest in new plants, thus raising its production capacity. But in a global economy the cars can be built elsewhere and imported at home. What is really needed is to convince the firm to invest at home.

- Second, how many people are available to work. The size of the labor force depends not only on demographic factors, such as the population growth rate, but also on people's willingness to enter the labor market rather than stay home.

- Third, technical progress, which determines how productive capital and labor are.

We call *structural reforms* all the policies that convince entrepreneurs to invest more (especially at home rather than abroad), people to work more, and technical progress to rise more rapidly.

These magic words—structural reforms, sometimes replaced by "structural policies" or "supply-side reforms"—are routinely advocated in all press communiqués at the end of G-20 and other economic policy summits. But which structural reforms really help? The list is long, and not all agree on the priorities. The most standard lists—the ones that we find in the standard publications of international organization such as the IMF and the Organization for Economic Cooperation and Development—include such things as the following:

- A flexible labor market with low hiring and firing costs, to facilitate the shift of labor toward growing sectors, and with salary increases better aligned with productivity growth.

- A reduction in barriers to international trade, as more trade is seen as improving economic efficiency. After Trump's election, however, pro-trade policies no longer feature prominently in G-20 communiqués.

- A reduction in red tape and bureaucratic obstacles to business.

- Lower taxation on labor and profits, offset by increased taxation on activities that cause externalities, that is, negative effects on others, such as polluting activities, or by cuts in less efficient public priority spending, although the emphasis on the need for lower taxation, at least in the advice of the international organizations, is less marked in countries where taxes are already below the advanced economies' average, such as the United States and Japan.

- More competition in goods and service markets, as more competition means more efficiency.

- Better education to improve human capital.

- Greater investment in infrastructure. Recently, the importance of infrastructural investment, either by the public sector or through public-private-partnerships, has been emphasized.

This list is quite generic and may therefore be disappointing. It is difficult to be more exciting because the specific structural reforms that are appropriate for each country vary depending on the specific country situation. But in general, the reforms recommended by most mainstream economists, and certainly the main international organizations, are those that lead to stronger economic incentives and competition, with a state that intervenes in the economy primarily through regulation and taxation aimed at creating a level playing field and correcting externalities. Economic incentives are necessary to invest more and better, to innovate more, and to work harder. These incentives, however, require a level playing field on which competitive forces can act and overcome lobbies and rent seeking, advantages that may arise from excessive regulation. Very often the U.S. economy provides the example for other countries—an attractive example, in light of the higher rate of growth experienced by the United States with respect to other advanced economies such as Japan and most European countries, which are hampered by various rigidities and excessive regulations. Even the 2008–09 crisis, which originated in the United States, has been overcome by the United States much more easily than by European economies, an additional proof of the former's economic flexibility and resilience.

Addressing the issue of what structural reforms can improve growth trends across advanced economies would require an entire book and extend beyond my expertise. That said, many advanced economies, especially in Europe, would benefit from moving toward more competition and more room for economic incentives, while the United States would benefit from a better recognition of the existence of market failures to be corrected through taxation and regulation. To give an example, energy taxes in the United States are far below what they should be, and their increase would allow some decline in other, more distortionary, taxes. But here I want to stress a different point, a point that is valid for all advanced economies— indeed, all economies: economists simply do not know enough to assess with a sufficient degree of precision how long it will take for structural reforms to have an impact on potential growth. What we do know is that structural reforms in the short run have a small to negative impact on economic growth and that it takes several years before their full positive impact is seen. Things can differ from country to country, but on average, this is what available studies show.[9]

Another problem is that structural reforms that make economies more competitive and enhance economic incentives do not benefit everybody, at least in the short run. Let's consider, for example, a reform that makes the labor market more flexible by making it easier to fire workers. It is probably good for the economy as a whole as it facilitates the shift of manpower toward new and expanding economic sectors. But its immediate effect is to lower the bargaining power of workers who are already employed, changing the balance between labor and capital in wage negotiations. This, together with other effects of liberalization measures, is likely to affect income distribution. Over the longer run, GDP may be higher as a whole, and perhaps for everybody, but in the short run there will be losers. Thus, many people will object to structural reforms of this kind, perhaps noting that northern European economies seem to work very efficiently, even with the state playing a much more intrusive role in the economy than in the United States. Given all these resistances, both approving structural reform legislation and implementing it are bound to be difficult and time-consuming, and may exhaust a government's political capital.

It makes sense, therefore, to be prudent in assessing whether higher potential growth can solve the public debt problem. In particular, it would not be credible, and might elicit an adverse market reaction, to base fiscal adjustment plans on optimistic assumptions about the effect that certain reforms can have on economic growth. In other words, structural reforms are needed, but governments should be prudent with respect to estimating their growth and tax revenue yield. The overall fiscal policy design proposed in chapter 15 (including the moderate fiscal austerity component) takes this into account.

Secular Stagnation

In case this heavy dose of realism has not been enough, here is another piece of bad news. After the 2008–09 crisis the whole world economy has not grown much. The average growth rate of the world economy between

2012 and 2016 was 3.3 percent, well below the 4.5 percent recorded during 2000–07. Growth in the earlier period, however, was probably inflated by developments and economic policies that led to the 2008–09 crisis. Thus it would be unrealistic to try to go back to those growth rates. Moreover, the growth rates of emerging economies are not too bad. They grew at an annual rate of 4.6 percent during 2012–16, above their growth rate in the thirty years before 2000 (4.3 percent). What is weak is the growth rate of advanced economies, which was just 1.6 percent during 2012–16, against 3.1 percent in the thirty years before 2000. Part of this decline is attributable to demographic forces: advanced economies' populations are not growing as rapidly as in the past. However, it is still remarkable that the growth rate is not higher in light of the super-expansionary monetary policies pursued in the last few years.

As discussed in chapter 9, the ineffectiveness of monetary policies could be explained by various factors: household and firms are still reducing the debt stock accumulated during the previous decade, and bank regulation has been tightened considerably, making it harder for banks to lend as easily as in the past. But many believe that low growth in advanced economies could be due to more persistent factors that could lead to a "secular stagnation." So secular stagnation theories have flourished in recent years, focusing on both demand and supply factors.

Larry Summers has argued that the main problem is a chronic lack of aggregate demand, the result not only of excessive debt accumulation in the past but also of the lower capital needs of expanding sectors.[10] As noted also by Governor of the Bank of Italy Ignazio Visco in his book *Perché i tempi stanno cambiando*, a digital startup does not require a large investment, which lowers the demand for investment goods in comparison with past trends.[11] Other economists, such as Bob Gordon (in his best seller *The Rise and Fall of American Growth*), have blamed the possible secular stagnation on lower productivity growth in the absence of sufficient technical progress: technical progress in the last few years has centered on the information and telecommunications sector, but technological advances in this sector do not seem to have had much impact on the economy's overall productivity. The "second machine age," to quote the title of another recent bestseller by Erik Brynjolfsson and Andrew McAfee, is promising more than it is delivering.[12]

The explanation of a possible secular stagnation that most worries me, however, focuses on the effects that changes in income distribution observed over the last thirty to thirty-five years are having on aggregate demand in advanced economies. Income distribution in many advanced economies has moved toward the rich since the beginning of the 1980s, reversing a trend that had been observed since the early twentieth century. In the United States, for example, the income of the richest 1 percent of the population now accounts for 20 percent of overall income, against 8 percent at the beginning of the 1980s and 18 percent in the early 1900s. Similar trends, although not as marked, have been observed in other countries. Thomas Piketty's *Capital in the Twenty-First Century* illustrates these trends in detail.[13]

We may or may not like more inequality in income distribution. But this is not my point. My point, in terms of growth, is that if the middle class loses too much purchasing power, aggregate demand structurally does not grow fast enough because no matter how hard they try, the very rich cannot consume enough to replace the declining demand from the middle class. To offset this insufficient demand, the approach followed during the 2000s, and to a less successful extent in the 2010s, has been to run expansionary monetary policies that would reduce interest rates and induce the middle class to borrow more. In other words, the average American family might have lower income but could continue consuming by borrowing more. Atif Mian and Amir Sufi's book *House of Debt*, illustrates well these trends, noting that the ratio between American households' debt and their income increased from 150 percent in 2000 to 210 percent in 2008.[14] From this point of view, the debt accumulation observed during the 2000s was not a random event but an inevitable consequence of the attempt to offset the lack of aggregate demand by the middle class through expansionary, debt-creating monetary policies. However, an increase in debt also leads to greater risk exposure: if for any reason interest rates start rising, the full burden of households' debt becomes apparent and leads to repayment difficulties. In turn, these difficulties can trigger a financial crisis, as they did in 2008–09. This is also the interpretation given to the 2008–09 crisis by Raghuram Rajan, former chief economist of the IMF and former governor of the Central Bank of India, in his book *Fault Lines*.[15]

Of course, it is possible to support aggregate demand also through expansionary fiscal policies. This, however, leads to an excessive accumulation of public debt, and in this case an economy becomes exposed to the risk of a lack of confidence in the ability of the government to repay its debt, one of the themes of this book. Moreover, the problem of lack of demand has been exacerbated by the low propensity of households to consume in some of the fastest-growing emerging market economies, such as China, where household income has greatly increased over the last two decades. Income distribution across countries has moved toward these economies, but this shift has not boosted aggregate demand sufficiently, as China's households' saving rate is quite low. Altogether, if we do not go back to a more balanced income distribution, we will have to choose between lower growth because of insufficient aggregate demand and growth instability as a result of exposure to risks arising from excessive debt accumulation. The choice is not an appealing one.

Should we not then try to correct income distribution? What has caused the shift in income distribution? I am afraid that, unfortunately, globalization is to a large extent responsible for the shift in income distribution. Why? In a market economy, the distribution of income between capital and labor depends on the relative availability of these two factors of production. The more workers are available, the cheaper labor becomes compared to capital. The entry into the world economy of countries like China and India—rich in labor and poor in capital—has led to a rapid increase in the ratio between available labor and available capital, and hence to a reduction in the remuneration of labor, especially lower-skilled labor. If so, it would then be difficult to correct income distribution without giving up the advantages of a globalized economy: despite the criticism levied against globalization by the new U.S. administration, most consumers do like buying cheaper stuff made in China. You could try to increase taxes on capital and the rich, but capital can move more quickly than labor from one country to another, escaping taxation, especially in a world where there are no effective approaches to coordinating taxation across countries. Moreover, who ultimately pays a tax is not necessarily the agent over which the tax is levied because prices (in this case of labor and capital) would adjust in response to taxation so as to offset the redistributional impact of taxation. And prices respond to the elasticities of demand and supply: the more capital is elastic to increases in tax rates, the more any attempt to tax it would be offset by changes in the relative remuneration of capital and labor.

In sum, various forces could lead, over the coming years and perhaps decades, to lower growth in advanced economies, thus making it more difficult to bring down public debt ratios.

An Optimistic Postscript

Before I conclude this chapter—which started with an optimistic "motherhood and apple pie" flavor and ended with secular stagnation fears—let me offer a glimmer of hope. In chapter 4, I noted that high public debt lowers potential growth. Not much attention has been paid so far to the possibility that the slowing of advanced economies' potential growth after the 2008–09 global recession owed precisely to the surge in public debt. And yet the estimated decline in potential output for the main advanced economies matches fairly accurately what was predicted by estimates of the effect of public debt on growth. The IMF has estimated that potential output growth declined between the precrisis period and the postcrisis period by 0.8 percent in the United States. The Kumar and Woo model cited in chapter 4 predicts that as a result of the rise in the public debt ratio, potential growth should have declined precisely by the same amount.[16] For the simple average of the fifteen largest advanced economies, the estimated decline in potential output growth is again 0.8 percent, close to the 0.5 percent decline predicted by the Kumar-Woo model. Despite the accuracy, some doubts may arise as to whether the impact of higher public debt on potential output growth in the postcrisis period could really be as high: what is missing are the symptoms that the channels through which high public debt would affect potential growth are operating, for example higher real interest rates, which would crowd out private investment. The impact of higher public debt may, however, be operating in more subtle ways, for example through expectations of future tax increases or the kind of crowding out through bank regulation (discussed in chapter 9) that would cause credit rationing.

Altogether, one can hope that if a process of reducing the public debt ratios is started in advanced economies, it could have a beneficial effect on potential output growth itself, and hence on fiscal revenues. This in turn would facilitate a faster decline in the debt ratio and so would start a self-reinforcing virtuous cycle that would lead to a faster decline in public debt and an acceleration in growth. But for all this to work, a modicum of fiscal austerity is also needed. It is time to take the final step in our long journey.

FIFTEEN

A Bit of Austerity

Austerity does not work. Period.

—*Mark Blyth*

In Spain, it worked. It was painful, but it worked.

—*Jesús García Aldaz*

I think growing an economy is a good way to help with a deficit, but ultimately, it's about fiscal discipline and responsible spending, and smart decisions.

—*Justin Trudeau*

Austerity is out of fashion, especially now that interest rates on government securities are still relatively low. Differing from the seemingly easier and painless solutions discussed in previous chapters, austerity appears painful and inconsistent with what ultimately really matters, GDP growth. And yet the term is rarely defined by those who criticize it, and has different meanings. Some use it to label draconian cuts in public spending or large tax increases, and hence sizable reductions in the fiscal deficit. Some use it to indicate any policy of deficit reduction, no matter how small. Some describe austerity as the absence of expansionary measures. And some anti-austerity politicians use the term simply to mean any fiscal policy that will prevent them from winning the next election.

This chapter clarifies the kind of fiscal policies that in my view are needed to bring about a gradual reduction in the public debt-to-GDP ratio. I argue that, if initiated soon enough, these policies would involve a moderate austerity that would not excessively penalize growth in the short run and would promote growth in the long run. In most cases, even in high public debt countries, such policies should be sufficient to reduce significantly the risk that the financial markets see public debt as a major threat to economic stability. But they need to be implemented without further delay, as the window of opportunity provided by low interest rates will not last forever.

The specific fiscal policies needed for each country will inevitably depend on country circumstances, such as the degree of exposure to speculative attacks from financial markets, the initial public debt level, and the current levels of public spending and taxation. Nevertheless, there are some general principles that should hold for any country that is undertaking a process of gradual fiscal adjustment where the benefits of gradualism could be reaped only by resisting the temptation of policy reversals or procrastination. To be specific, I will show how these general principles could be turned into a policy prescription in the case of my country, Italy, one of the countries with the highest public debt-to-GDP ratio in the world.

General Principles for a Gradual Fiscal Adjustment

A fiscal adjustment is not like quitting smoking. Some say that fiscal adjustment can only be done abruptly, by a frontloaded massive dose of spending cuts and tax increases or by defaulting on public debt. Otherwise the risk of reversals, of "policy fatigue," is just too high. With massive frontloading, there is no turning back.

Abrupt action may work for smoking cessation, but it is not necessarily applicable to fiscal adjustment. There have been many cases of gradual reduction in the public debt ratio achieved through a combination of fiscal adjustment and growth, as will be discussed below.

A gradual strengthening of the primary balance and an initial decline in the public debt ratio are, however, exposed to the risk of policy reversals. One way to reduce this risk is to introduce a credible medium-term fiscal framework, a path of medium-term fiscal objectives announced by the government that will guide policymaking over time. This medium-term fiscal framework can be supported by a formal set of fiscal rules or it can be supported by processes that make it clear and transparent when policies are deviating from their initially stated course, and why (the next chapter looks more closely at fiscal rules and other institutional devices in support of gradual fiscal adjustment).

A medium-term fiscal framework needs to:

- Be based on relatively conservative growth projections to be credible. Structural reforms can help, but, as argued, we just do not know enough about how long it will take them to increase growth. So one has to be cautious.

- Define clearly a medium-term target path for the primary balance and the overall fiscal balance that needs to be achieved and maintained over time and that is consistent with a gradual decline in the public debt ratio to a long-term level that keeps the country resilient to shocks. The appropriate long-term debt target depends on country circumstances, particularly the country's vulnerability to shocks, but, as a rule of thumb, for advanced economies a debt ratio of 40 to 60 percent of GDP seems to be a reasonable target (as discussed in chapter 6).

- Envisage a pace of decline in the public debt ratio large enough to reassure financial markets that it is not the result of random developments. It should be seen as a trend that cannot be easily reversed by shocks. Also, in this case, the speed needs to be country-specific, with the urgency of the fiscal adjustment taken into account.

- Define the tools needed to achieve the primary balance target, and with sufficient specificity, even if legislating all the measures ex ante is unlikely.

- Be clear about the (limited) circumstances in which deviations from the plan would be allowed. The extent to which macroeconomic shocks could justify a deviation from the targets should also be country-specific. But one cannot expect, even in countries where fiscal adjustment needs are less pressing, that any cyclical slowing down should lead to a revision of the fiscal framework. Fiscal policy cannot be used as flexibly as monetary policy because of the political difficulty of tightening compared with relaxing it. However, for most countries, the automatic stabilizers should be allowed to operate, up to a point.

What does it mean exactly to "let the automatic stabilizers operate"? The economy is subject to ups and downs. Apart from very unusual crises, such as the one that hit the world in 2008–09, GDP moves in cycles around its medium term-trend. The trend is determined by potential growth, while the short-term cycle is determined by the relative strength of aggregate demand over time: in some periods demand rises faster, in others more slowly. In weaker phases of the economic cycle, GDP is below its potential level, and tax revenues are relatively weaker (some spending, for example for unemployment, may also go up). In stronger phases, GDP is above potential and revenues are relatively stronger (and some spending is also lower). So, depending on the phase of the cycle, the fiscal deficit may be temporarily weaker or temporarily stronger. By "letting the automatic stabilizers operate," I mean allowing the fiscal balance to be temporarily weaker when the economy slows down. This will not affect trend developments as long as the fiscal balance is relatively stronger when GDP is (temporarily) above its potential level. If instead we were to focus rigidly on pursuing the original fiscal targets when the economy slowed down, we would accentuate the economic cycle because, when revenues slow as a result of a temporary recession, the government would have to cut spending to achieve the original fiscal target, and that step would make the economy even weaker.

This kind of flexibility does not jeopardize the credibility of the fiscal adjustment because it is self-correcting: when the economy recovers, revenues will rise, and the fiscal deficit will go back to its original trend. Fiscal policy, once the route is set based on the initial medium-term fiscal policy plan, is on autopilot: no additional intervention is needed. One caveat: cyclical deviations of fiscal balances from the targets should be allowed only up to a point, as large deviations of GDP from the original path may suggest that the original GDP path was just too optimistic or that the potential GDP growth trend has changed, which would imply the need for a fiscal correction.

Such an approach seems appropriate for many high-debt countries. Some, those with higher fiscal credibility and less exposed to the risks of a speculative attack, could perhaps afford a more active fiscal policy not just accommodating the effect of the economic cycle on the fiscal accounts but involving the active use of discretionary interventions to try to further offset cyclical shocks. That could be quite dangerous, however, as in general, discretionary interventions are not self-correcting and the risk that spending increases or tax cuts are not reversed in a timely fashion would be significant. Only under exceptional circumstances—a major recession, for example—should discretionary fiscal action be allowed for countries engaged in public debt reduction strategies. In other words, Keynes is good, but only for major macroeconomic shocks.

A Medium-Term Fiscal Adjustment Plan in Practice:
The Case of Italy

As an illustration of the principles just discussed, let's look at how, in practice, public debt could be reduced in Italy. How much "austerity" is needed? I draw the following scenario from my book *Il macigno* (The boulder), that, while a bit outdated, will give you an idea of the approach I would suggest.[1]

The basic idea, in line with what was discussed in the previous pages, would be to freeze primary spending in real terms at the 2016 level and save all the revenues coming from the increase in GDP until the budget is balanced. Balancing the budget is a reasonable medium-term goal for Italy, in keeping with its high public debt. Achieving and maintaining a balanced budget, net of cyclical effects, was introduced as a key fiscal rule in the Italian constitution at the end of 2011 and is in line with Italy's commitments within the euro zone. Freezing primary spending in real terms means that spending, net of interest payments, would increase over time only in line with inflation. Because in the meantime, government revenues will tend to increase in proportion to nominal GDP, and hence faster in the presence of positive real GDP growth, the primary and the overall balance will improve over time until the overall budget is balanced. With a balanced budget, public debt will stop rising in euro terms and the public debt ratio will decline over time.[2]

In 2016 the fiscal deficit was equal to 2.4 percent of GDP. How long would it take before a balanced budget, that is, a zero deficit, was achieved? That depends on the real GDP growth rate (the inflation rate is not relevant because it affects equally revenues and spending), as well as on interest rates. In the official growth scenario envisaged when *Il macigno* was published (projecting a GDP growth rate averaging 1.5 percent during 2016–19), the budget would have been balanced by 2019. Since then, actual GDP growth has fallen somewhat below what was expected and the official growth projections for 2016–19 are now averaging 1.1 percent. In keeping with the general principle put forward earlier of allowing deviations from the target in case of relatively contained deviations of GDP growth from the initial projections, this means that it may take a bit longer to achieve a balanced budget, but the longer duration would not significantly affect the long-term dynamics of the public debt ratio.

Once the budget has been balanced, it should remain balanced until the public debt has fallen to the desired long-term level, except for what I called the effect of the economic cycle. In other words, it should be kept balanced in "cyclically adjusted" or "structural" terms.[3] The primary surplus would have to be maintained at a level of 4 to 4.5 percent of GDP over the next decade, while it could decline gradually thereafter as the debt level declines.

How fast will the debt-to-GDP ratio decline once a balanced budget has been achieved? As public debt in euro terms would not change, the public debt ratio would decline because of the increase in nominal GDP, and so the speed of the decline would depend on how fast nominal GDP grew. I think it is reasonable to assume a nominal GDP growth rate of some 3 percent per year for the medium term, let's say 1.5 to 1.75 percent of inflation plus 1.25 to 1.5 percent of real growth. The former is in line with the European Central Bank's inflation target of close to but below 2 percent. The latter is higher than the growth rate of the Italian economy over the last few years, which was affected by the two shocks of the 2008–09 global crisis and the 2011–12 euro-zone crisis, but is slightly below the average GDP growth rate in the ten years before the 2008–09 crisis (1.5 percent).

With a nominal GDP growth rate of 3 percent, a balanced budget would drive down the public debt ratio steadily over time. The ratio would fall below 90 percent of GDP in about 2030 and below 60 percent by the mid-2040s. It would then be a slow decline, but it could be accelerated with the help of privatization revenues, which in the above scenario are assumed to be zero after 2019.

Something else should be recalled, and this is important not just for Italy but for all countries involved in a process of public debt reduction. The shortcomings arising from high public debt—exposure to crisis risk and lower potential growth—are significantly reduced if the public debt ratio, while still high, is on a declining trend. As discussed in chapter 3, a crisis on the government paper markets primarily occurs when public debt is not only high but rising. If public debt is declining at a sufficient speed, it is less likely to start rising even in the presence of a negative economic shock. Moreover, the impact of high public debt on potential growth is much reduced if public debt is rising (see chapter 4). So, while the decline in debt will be slow, countries will benefit from a debt reduction strategy much earlier than one might guess simply by looking at the debt-to-GDP ratio.

How "Austere" Is the Proposed Approach, and Is It Consistent with Growth?

The strategy proposed above does involve some degree of austerity. The revenues from the increase in real GDP are not spent but saved, as long as it takes to reach a balanced budget. Probably this involves somewhat lower GDP growth in the short run compared to a scenario in which public spending rises in line with potential output growth and the government securities market remain quiet. If primary spending were allowed to grow every year instead of being kept constant, aggregate demand and GDP would probably grow somewhat faster. However, this gain would be limited. First, there is the risk that, with lower fiscal adjustment, uncertainty over the solvency of the Italian fiscal accounts would increase, thus worsening the private investment environment and lowering Italy's potential growth. Second, any possibly short-term loss in GDP growth would have to be weighed against the reduced risk of a rollover crisis in the government paper market that would have devastating effects on the Italian economy. In other words, in the absence of a fiscal adjustment, the government securities market may not remain quiet. Third, the drag on aggregate demand would last only until the budget is balanced. Thereafter public spending could resume growing in line with potential GDP. On average, throughout the economic cycle the budget would be balanced, but, as discussed, deficits would be allowed in a downturn, as the automatic stabilizers would be allowed to operate, as long as they were offset by surpluses in cyclical upswings. This would help stabilize aggregate demand.

What about the long-term impact of keeping a balanced budget? Would balancing the budget reduce potential growth through supply-side effects? With respect to the current situation, balancing the budget in Italy implies raising the primary surplus from the current level of about 1.5 percent of GDP to a level above 4 percent of GDP, and keeping it there for several years. This is a common problem of countries with high debt that attempt a gradual decline in the debt ratio: keeping a primary surplus as high as what is needed to lower the debt ratio means keeping taxes at a higher level, or spending at a lower level, than would be required just to stabilize public debt at higher levels. Would this not penalize potential growth?

Once more, let's think about our car firm. If taxes are kept high to lower public debt, or if the government does not provide good infrastructure because it must spend less, the firm may decide to invest abroad. We have already discussed why high public debt can lower potential growth: high debt requires high taxes to service interest payments even if we just want to stabilize the debt ratio. But lowering the debt ratio requires raising taxes to an even higher level than would be needed just to stabilize the debt ratio. Would this not make things worse? Of course, this situation would not last forever, as eventually debt would reach the desired lower level and taxes could be cut. But taxes would be cut only in the long term, while initially taxes would be higher: in present value terms, the higher initial taxes might even weigh more. This seems to create a puzzle for supporters of gradual, orthodox fiscal adjustment, as noted recently by three IMF economists, Raphael Espinoza, Atish R. Ghosh, and Jonathan D. Ostry, who concluded that countries with a public debt that is not so high as to cause major risks of rollover crises, as is currently the case with the United States, could reasonably prefer to keep public debt at relatively high levels to avoid the costs in terms of potential growth arising from the adjustment process.[4]

I do not agree with this position, at least as a general proposition, for various reasons.

First, as recognized also by the three IMF economists, countries like Italy remain exposed to the risk of rollover crises of the kind experienced in 2011–12.

Second, lowering public debt increases potential growth not only because of lower tax rates but also because of lower real interest rates, which would encourage more private investment, something that the three IMF economists do not consider.

Third, the goal of keeping a balanced budget could catalyze cuts in nonproductive public spending that may not have materialized if the fiscal targets had been less ambitious.

Finally, another recent paper by two other IMF economists—one might think that the debate on these issues within the IMF is quite intense these days—notes that the Espinoza-Ghosh-Ostry argument does not take into account the nature of the shocks affecting the fiscal accounts: fiscal accounts are subject to large negative shocks (wars, sharp recessions), and if public debt were not gradually reduced in relatively good times, the average public debt level would be higher than it would otherwise be, thus requiring a higher tax level, which would penalize growth.

Be that as it may, to assess the feasibility in terms of growth prospects of primary surpluses of, say, four percentage points, one should ask, is there anything inherently bad for an economy to keep a primary surplus of 4 percent rather than, say, 2 percent? Put in these terms, the difference looks big. But let's look at it from the point of view of total primary spending and revenue ratios. Italy's primary spending is equal to about 45 percent of GDP. Could one possibly argue that it would be unsustainable for the Italian economy to, in the long run, keep primary spending at 43 percent of GDP, especially if you take into account the possibility of cutting the still large unproductive spending?

There is a final argument in favor of the sustainability of a gradual debt reduction strategy: as discussed in chapter 4, based on the experience of other countries, a reduction in the public debt ratio should raise the economy's medium-term potential growth rate. This should not only reduce over time the primary surplus needed to lower public debt at a certain speed but should also make it easier, from a political point of view, to maintain a certain level of the primary surplus. Moreover, as public debt declines, the burden of interest payments will also decline, and this factor too will make it possible to lower over time the primary surplus needed to bring down public debt. Finally, if the decline in public debt is also accompanied, as it should be, by a decline in interest rates on public debt (because of the lower risk of a rollover crisis), the required primary surplus will further decline. This is the kind of virtuous circle that Italy and other high-debt countries need to activate to solve the public debt problem.

Are There Precedents of Successful Gradual Debt Reduction Strategies?

Another objection to the gradual debt reduction strategy is that there are few cases of countries that kept a primary surplus as high a 4 percent for a long time. It is indeed not too common, but also not unprecedented. Some of my former colleagues in the Fiscal Affairs Department of the IMF studied the main cases of reduction in the public debt ratio in the post–World War II period in a sample of fifty-three advanced and emerging economies. They found that, out of twenty-three cases of strong debt reduction, in eight the primary surplus exceeded 4 percent for at least ten years.

If we focus specifically on advanced economies involved in fiscal adjustment strategies, we find that over the past thirty years, nine advanced economies (more than one-fourth of all advanced economies) managed to lower their public debt-to-GDP ratio by at least twenty percentage points at a speed of at least two percentage points sustained for at least eight years. These countries succeeded in lowering their public debt ratios, in the context of a growing economy, by running for prolonged periods of time large primary surpluses, averaging 4.5 percent of GDP.[5] For example, Belgium managed to lower its debt ratio by some fifty percentage points between 1994, when debt stood at 134 percent of GDP, and 2007. After doing so, it was fairly well shielded by the speculative attacks that several European countries suffered in the following years.

The key ingredient in these cases was the saving of some of the resources that came from higher growth to allow a gradual strengthening of the primary balance: spending as a percentage of GDP did often decline, but spending was typically not cut in real terms, at least not over the medium term. That approach requires, of course, a modicum of growth. To be fair, the growth rates experienced by these countries were higher than the one that, in the context of diminished growth prospects, now seems likely for advanced economies: for example, Belgium's growth rate during its 1994–2007 debt reduction episode averaged 2.5 percent. But a strategy of gradual debt reduction does not necessarily require high growth to succeed: growth rates were higher in debt reduction episodes in the past simply because growth in all advanced countries was higher. But there is no evidence that success was affected by the level of growth: in particular, in the nine advanced economies that managed to lower their public debt ratios for a sustained period of time, there was no correlation between the level of growth and the level of the primary surplus that was maintained over time.

Past evidence, in any case, can be misleading. Relatively few cases of large, prolonged primary surpluses have been observed in the past, perhaps just because in recent decades public debt was not as high, and so it was not necessary to maintain large primary surpluses over time.

Cut Spending or Raise Taxes?

In the adjustment scenario I just described for Italy, the burden of the adjustment falls on public spending. No increases in tax rates are proposed, and tax revenues increase simply because of the increase in GDP over time. Of course, if it were deemed necessary also to cut tax rates (as I think it should be in Italy), then it would be necessary to reduce primary spending in real terms. Would a different strategy to improve the primary balance be possible? Should Italy or other countries rely on tax increases rather than on public expenditure containment?

In deciding whether to contain spending or to raise taxes, two considerations are relevant. The first is the effect that certain tax increases or spending cuts can have on aggregate demand and hence on GDP in the short run. Not all tightening measures reduce aggregate demand by the same amount. For example, if the government spends less in purchasing goods and services directly from the private sector, there is a direct impact on production. If instead the government cuts transfers to households, for example pension entitlements, households will spend less but probably will also reduce their saving to maintain their standard of living relatively unaffected, and so aggregate spending will decline less than the initial cut in government spending. The same would happen for tax cuts, whose impact on aggregate demand would probably be muffled by lower saving.[6] In principle, and from a short-term perspective, it would be better to find fiscal adjustment measures whose impact on aggregate demand is minimal. It would be nice to find such measures, but my experience is that economists still do not know enough on the relative impact of various fiscal measures on aggregate demand to fine-tune the composition of a fiscal adjustment package based on their effect on aggregate demand in the short run. In any case, these are indeed short-term effects, which I do not think should drive the decision on the composition of fiscal adjustment measures.

The second consideration relates to the impact that spending cuts or tax increases would have on medium-term potential growth. Here also economists do not know too much, but perhaps something a bit more precise can be said, and in any case, longer-term considerations are more important. If some public expenditures are clearly wasteful, then it would be better to cut them rather than raise taxes, which in general distorts economic behaviors. Waste in public spending is more likely to exist the larger primary spending is with respect to GDP. It seems to me that most European countries are in such a situation, and that is why I believe that for those countries, fiscal adjustment measures should focus primarily on the spending side. I am not among those who believe that it is always better to cut public spending rather than raise taxes. The adjustment chosen depends on initial conditions. For example, in the United States, where some taxes, for example on energy, are quite low compared with those of other countries, part of the fiscal adjustment should be made on the revenue side. But in most European countries, where taxes are already high, the adjustment should focus on the spending side.

A One-Off Wealth Levy?

Because of the time it takes for gradual fiscal adjustment to lower GDP considerably, in high public debt countries it is not infrequent to hear discussions of more drastic measures, such as a one-off large levy on wealth. Of course, many countries levy recurrent taxes on some form of wealth, most typically real estate, and they also have relatively small taxes on wealth triggered by special events, such as inheritance taxes. But here I am talking about a levy on wealth large enough to bring down public debt by a sizable amount. Taxes of this kind have been proposed, for example in Italy in 2010, and have been quite common in economic history, having featured in Europe after World War I and in Germany and Japan after World War II.[7]

Strangely, wealth levies are often assumed to be a complete alternative to more orthodox forms of fiscal adjustment, and yet, as a first approximation, a wealth levy, like other forms of fiscal adjustment, would also have tightening effects on the economy in the short run. There are, however, important differences, which the supporters of this approach often underscore. First, a tax levy taxes wealth, and therefore, by definition, "the rich," who can afford a larger sacrifice. Second, the rich might not alter their lifestyle and might continue to consume, so the impact on aggregate demand might be smaller. Third, a wealth levy introduced suddenly leaves little room for circumvention, although economic history tells us that delays occur in practice, thus reducing considerably yields from initial expectations. Fourth—and this is probably the most important advantage—a tax levy, if perceived as really one-off, does not distort future economic behavior, contrary to what happens with recurrent taxes, which affect incentives to work and to invest. Finally, the impact on debt of a tax levy would be felt immediately, whereas other, more orthodox measures would have to be sustained over time and hence would be exposed to the risk of "adjustment fatigue" and prone to policy reversals.

But there are also some negative aspects of a one-off wealth levy. Those who had to pay the tax might suffer a liquidity squeeze: you own a beautiful house but you may not have enough cash to pay the tax, a problem that could be even more severe in countries where borrowing against the value of your house is not as easy as in the United States. Moreover, in many countries the problem is exacerbated by the fact that households' wealth is mostly real estate wealth. Finally, some of the key advantages of a wealth levy would arise only if it was really regarded as being one-off. But to be really regarded as such, it would probably have to be quite large, and hence less politically feasible and more likely to create liquidity problems.

Altogether, a wealth tax should not be completely ruled out as a possible solution to the public debt problem; and certainly it is better than public debt repudiation, which is tax on a specific form of wealth, that invested in government bonds (see chapter 10). But I would be cautious: its benefits and costs must be carefully evaluated against other forms of fiscal adjustment.

Postscript: Is There Still Time?

While this book is being finalized, and in the context of still relatively low interest rates on public debt, fiscal adjustment is slowing down in several countries in Europe with respect to original plans. In the case of Italy, the proposed strategy of keeping real spending constant is not being followed for 2017. While tougher adjustment is promised for 2018–19, fiscal plans have been relaxed with respect to previous commitments. This delays the decline in the public debt ratio with respect to the scenarios envisaged earlier in the chapter but does not fundamentally alter the public debt trajectory as long as procrastination is not indefinite. Interest rates have started edging up, and the time available before they might start rising rapidly is not much. As I have mentioned, it is important that fiscal adjustment proceed while interest rates are low to avoid subjecting the economy to the pressure of both monetary and fiscal tightening when interest rates inevitably rise.

SIXTEEN

Institutional Fiscal Constraints

I think the whole issue of a debt ceiling makes no sense to me whatsoever. Anybody who is remotely adroit at arithmetic doesn't need a debt ceiling to tell you where you are.

—Alan Greenspan

Bringing down public debt will not be easy. It will take a long time, and the temptation to declare victory prematurely will be strong. One thing that could help is to set up institutional constraints (legally binding rules or less formal constraints) to guide fiscal policy over time and make it transparent when it deviates from its stated course. Institutional fiscal constraints don't replace a culture of fiscal rectitude, which is really the decisive element in bringing down public debt. They are neither a sufficient nor a necessary condition to bring down public debt. Yet they can help by fostering a culture of fiscal rectitude, and it is worth looking at them in more detail.

Why Should Countries Tie Their Fiscal Hands through Fiscal Institutions?

Let's consider a country with its own currency and fiscal policy. Why should such a country impose institutional constraints on its fiscal policy management? Why, for example, did Tony Blair's Labour government introduce fiscal rules that limited its discretion in deciding every year its fiscal deficit and public debt targets when it reached power in the United Kingdom in the middle of the 1990s? And why do many countries do it?

They do it to enhance the predictability of fiscal policy and hence their credibility in managing it wisely: following certain rules makes fiscal policy more predictable and lowers the risk that it will be used to achieve contingent goals, especially electoral goals, rather than to pursue long-term objectives and ensure that the state is able to repay its creditors. Fiscal rules may also help governments resist pressure from lobbies, thus anchoring fiscal policy. If a government has fiscal credibility, it can borrow at lower interest rates, which is good for the whole economy.

Were it not for this credibility problem, full discretion in managing fiscal policy would be optimal. Suppose, for example, that the government expects the economy to weaken next year. To boost the economy, the government could plan an increase in public spending. Financial markets should not worry about the related increase in the deficit because it would be a temporary increase, one that the government would promptly reverse once economic conditions improved. But how could one know the real motivation for the increase in public spending? Next year there may also be elections, and an increase in spending could help the government win them. And even if no elections are slated, how can we be sure that increased public spending today will be offset by lower spending tomorrow, when economic conditions improve, rather than lead to a permanent increase in deficits and debt? It is precisely to provide some certainty about future fiscal policy decisions that many governments and parliaments have introduced institutional constraints anchoring fiscal policy and expectations.

There are two basic approaches to fiscal institutional constraints. The first one is to legislate, possibly at the constitutional level, formal rules affecting key fiscal variables, such as the fiscal deficit, public debt, public spending, or, less frequently, the tax pressure. Tony Blair's government actually introduced two fiscal rules from the very beginning of its term, perhaps to fight the preconception that Labour, as a leftist party, did not care about the public accounts. The first rule required the budget, net of investment spending, to balance on average over one full economic cycle, that is, incling a recession and an expansion. The second rule required public debt to be below 40 percent of GDP, a much tighter constraint than the 60 percent imposed by EU fiscal rules. Scores of other countries have fiscal rules.[1]

A second approach—one followed, for example, by Australia and New Zealand—aims at strengthening fiscal credibility without formal rules but by publishing medium-term fiscal frameworks or plans extending three to four years ahead, plans that are considered binding by the government. Again, the idea is to make fiscal policy more predictable. A fiscal plan involves a bit more flexibility, at least ex ante, than a fiscal rule because it allows the government more freedom to decide the pace of fiscal adjustment over the next few years. However, once the plan is defined, it does involve, ex post, some constraint on fiscal policy.

Adopting a fiscal rule or a fiscal framework does not, of course, ensure credibility. A fiscal rule is often introduced by a law, which can be amended later. Amendment would be more difficult if the rule were embodied in the constitution, but even constitutions can be changed. And if there are no clear legal consequences for breaching the rule, it can simply be ignored. Rules often have to be interpreted, and governments are quite good at interpreting them to suit their needs. The German constitution, for example, before the latest amendments introducing a quasi-balanced budget, required the government to balance the budget net of investment spending, but this requirement was routinely violated without consequences. The United States has a simple fiscal rule: public debt cannot exceed a certain ceiling, expressed in dollar terms, but this ceiling is periodically lifted, though only after lengthy negotiations between the two sides of Congress. Informal fiscal frameworks can be changed even more easily than fiscal rules. Thus, institutional constraints are not a panacea, but they do represent an obstacle that governments and parliaments have to overcome if they want to implement riskier fiscal policies.

Fiscal Rules in the Euro Zone

Looking at euro-zone fiscal rules affords an opportunity to discuss more closely the trade-off between predictability or simplicity of fiscal rules and their flexibility to respond to unexpected shocks.

Euro-zone fiscal rules are a controversial topic. It must be Germany's fault, many economists and noneconomists believe, if Europe is imposing ironclad fiscal rules, the cornerstone of European austerity. The Maastricht Treaty, the Fiscal Compact, and the Stability and Growth Pact, the main agreements defining the fiscal rules for euro-zone members, must have been written by a Nordic hand that did not understand that rigid rules do not allow fiscal policy to be used in a smart way, with the ultimate goal the welfare of the people. This is a view strongly held by several American economists as well. In 2012 Joseph Stiglitz called the Fiscal Compact a "suicide pact." In the same year, Paul Krugman wrote about Europe's economic suicide.[2] And in the words of Alexis Tsipras, Greece's prime minister: "Austerity is not part of the European treaties; democracy and the principle of popular sovereignty are."[3]

However, almost all economic areas using a single currency impose fiscal rules on their members. The most obvious case relates to the rules that exist within a unitary state (which is also an economic area with a single currency) and constrain the fiscal flexibility of subnational governments. In almost all countries, for example, the deficits of municipalities or provinces are constrained by national fiscal rules. In federal states (such as the United States, Germany, or Canada) there are fiscal rules for states, lander, and provinces. We should not be surprised, therefore, if there are fiscal rules within the euro zone.

The special importance of having fiscal rules in common currency areas arises from a basic fact: the temptation to conduct irresponsible fiscal policies is much stronger for currency union members than for countries with their own currency because in currency areas, those who commit fiscal crimes may not be punished by financial markets. Let's see why.

In countries with their own currency, fiscal profligacy has consequences: sooner or later interest rates will go up, and voters may not like it. If the central bank prevents interest rates from going up by printing money to finance the government, inflation will rise, and voters may not like this either. All this reduces the risk of imprudent fiscal policies.

But in a monetary union, these inhibitors lose at least part of their effectiveness. If a currency union member increases its deficit, financial markets may not penalize it with higher interest rates because they may expect other members of the currency union to bail it out. In the case of the euro zone, the Maastricht Treaty prohibited any bailout, but eventually other member countries did come to the aid of Greece, Portugal, and Ireland. Therefore, in addition to the no-bailout clause, the Maastricht Treaty envisaged as an additional safeguard the introduction of fiscal rules, although these did not always work, as we will soon see.

The general problem is that when a country is a member of a currency area, its actions can damage other members. The costs of inappropriate fiscal behaviors are spread out over the entire monetary union rather than being borne just by the irresponsible country. This situation encourages all countries to maintain a larger deficit than they would have had they not shared their currency with other countries. As a result of higher deficits in the whole area, either interest rates will be higher or the pressure on the common central bank to print more money will increase, thus jeopardizing price stability. Hence the need for fiscal rules to protect the common currency from the risk of higher inflation. It is therefore entirely proper for the euro zone to have fiscal rules.

Euro-zone fiscal rules are messy. They are summarized by the Vade Mecum on the Stability and Growth Pact.[4] The Latin expression *vade mecum* ("come with me") suggests a lean document, one that you can take with you wherever you go. Instead, the European Vade Mecum is a 115-page document that, because it was published in 2013, does not include some important clarifications introduced in January 2015. The rules are complex partly because when you do not fully trust your partners—and I am afraid this is a real problem in Europe—you tend to codify everything in the most minute detail. But the rules are also complicated because they try to allow for some flexibility in responding to macroeconomic shocks. Indeed, there is a lot of misunderstanding in this respect: European rules are not as rigid as their critics argue.

With some simplifications, two main rules have existed since the formation of the euro zone. The first one is that the overall fiscal deficit should never exceed 3 percent of GDP. The second one is that public debt should not exceed 60 percent of GDP, and if it does, it should be declining "at a satisfactory pace." Why these numbers? It is not rocket science. In light of the evidence discussed in chapters 3 and 4, a public debt ratio of 60 percent of GDP does not seem to involve major risks, at least in advanced economies. In any case—and this is perhaps the most relevant factor—the debt ratio when the Maastricht Treaty was signed in the early 1990s was about 60 percent for the most "virtuous" large countries, such as Germany. And a deficit of 3 percent of GDP (trust me on the arithmetic of this computation), if maintained over time, is consistent with a debt ratio of 60 percent if nominal GDP is growing by 5 percent every year—something the European economies were hoping to achieve at that time.

While there were two rules, for a long time only the deficit rule really mattered, because how fast public debt should have declined to be declining "at a satisfactory pace" in the countries where it exceeded 60 percent of GDP was not clarified until recently.

The deficit rule was taken more seriously. Violating it implied the start of an "excessive deficit procedure" that, in principle, could lead to the imposition of sanctions if the offending country was not able to bring the deficit below 3 percent within a specific time frame. But the rule was frequently violated: between 1999 and 2007 it was violated in thirty-four instances, and in no case did this lead to sanctions. In practice, the time that was granted to offending countries to bring the deficit back below 3 percent was long enough to allow all countries to avoid sanctions. In some cases— the most notorious ones being those of France and Germany in 2003—the excessive deficit procedure was not even started because the political body that was expected to make the decision, the European Council (composed of the prime ministers of the member countries), was not willing to approve the recommendation made by the European Commission (the "government" of the European Union). On the contrary, after that episode, the fiscal rules were relaxed in 2005, something that is sometimes recalled by other countries when Germany complains too loudly that the European fiscal rules are not respected. In sum, during the past decade the European fiscal rules were not really ironclad, though fiscal developments probably would have been worse without them.

Things changed a bit with the 2011–12 euro-zone crisis. In exchange for Germany's willingness to support the countries in crisis, and recognizing that fiscal rules had to be taken more seriously, the euro-zone countries introduced three changes to the euro-zone fiscal framework. First, what was meant by debt declining "at a satisfactory pace" was clarified, which made the debt rule applicable in practice.[5] Second, the decision process leading to the initiation of an excessive deficit procedure was changed, if not dramatically, to increase its automaticity with respect to political decisions. Third, new rules were introduced to affect the fiscal deficit even when it was below 3 percent, the so-called preventive arm of the Stability and Growth Pact. The idea was that if 3 percent was a ceiling, in normal times the deficit should be well below that ceiling, to allow the deficit to increase during bad times without violating the 3 percent ceiling. Thus, each country was given a "medium-term objective" for the deficit that was expected to be achieved and maintained over time. Finally, a rule regulating public spending was also introduced.

Once again, this sounds very rigid and prescriptive, but several elements of flexibility were also introduced. First of all, most European fiscal rules are now computed with respect to a deficit corrected for cyclical factors, thus permitting a larger deficit if the economy slows down, one exception being the 3 percent deficit ceiling, still defined in headline (nonadjusted) terms.[6] Moreover, additional flexibility margins are granted—even in defining the targets of the cyclically adjusted deficit—for countries whose GDP is below its potential level and for those that are undertaking structural reforms or are increasing public investment. The most significant point, however, is that no country has ever been sanctioned for not meeting the European rules, even if some, at least borderline cases, certainly emerged.

The bottom line is that European fiscal rules are not as rigid as they seem. Indeed, it is not at all clear to me that, in their absence, euro-zone countries could run more expansionary fiscal policies. What is really constraining some of these countries is their high public debt and the risk of possible market reactions.

Fiscal Transparency and Fiscal Councils

The working of both approaches to institutional constraints on fiscal policy—fiscal rules and fiscal frameworks—can be enhanced by increasing fiscal transparency. The main idea behind this is that the more the public knows about fiscal developments, the more it will be able to evaluate whether fiscal policy is being managed in a way that is consistent with its stated purposes. Of course, all this works only if the goal of having the fiscal accounts in order is commonly held by the population. But assuming that it is, the pressure of public opinion can be exercised only if the fiscal accounts are sufficiently transparent. In many countries engaged in a process of fiscal adjustment, this has meant increased attention to publishing clear information on the fiscal accounts. The IMF has often pointed out how high fiscal transparency is often accompanied by better management of fiscal policy and an improvement in governments' credit ratings.[7]

Fiscal accounts are not easy to read, however, so the strengthening of fiscal institutions in many countries has also included the setting up of bodies—often called fiscal councils—in charge of monitoring fiscal developments and, sometimes more specifically, the implementation of fiscal rules. They are typically independent or nonpartisan bodies—that is, independent from political forces. Sometimes these bodies were not set up specifically for the purpose of providing independent views on fiscal developments but have, over time, acquired that role, as happened with the Congressional Budget Office in the United States. More often they were created with that specific mandate, such as the many fiscal councils set up in the euro zone in recent years.

Fiscal councils are, in principle, made up of independent experts, often chosen by a consensus decision by government and opposition political forces to ensure that they are indeed seen as unbiased. A more detailed discussion of how fiscal councils work in practice can be found in an IMF publication.[8] My impression is that, in practice, their effectiveness varies considerably across countries, depending on the extent to which they are truly independent, on the personality of the members of the council, and on the resources at their disposal, which may range from a handful of people to a cast of hundreds (the CBO in the United States employs 235 people). In general, however, fiscal councils are useful institutions that can help in promoting the culture of fiscal rectitude necessary to keep public debt at appropriate levels.

Conclusion: The Unbearable Lightness of Public Debt

A national debt, if it is not excessive, will be to us a national blessing.

—*Alexander Hamilton*

I hope Milan Kundera will forgive me for paraphrasing the title of his famous novel, *The Unbearable Lightness of Being*, for this final chapter summarizing the main messages of this book. I thought the paraphrase captured well the puzzle that advanced economies are currently facing: public debt has surged to levels that, in the past few centuries, had been reached only as a result of major wars. Yet there have been no dire consequences except in a few European countries in 2011–12, whose problems many blame on the shortcomings of the euro zone's monetary and fiscal institutional architecture rather than on public debt per se. So public debt is heavy from a quantitative point of view but appears light at present in terms of its consequences, a phenomenon underscored by the very low rates at which most governments are currently borrowing from eager investors.

This book casts doubts on this reassuring picture. The current apparent lightness of public debt is deceptive, and if the problem is disregarded, it will sooner or later turn into an unbearable burden. Hamilton emphasized that national debt should not be excessive. I am afraid the current level of public debt is indeed excessive in several countries.

But the book also has a reassuring message. First, the risks and costs that countries face as a result of high public debt differ from country to country. Countries with the same public debt-to-GDP ratio do not face the same hurdles: a lot depends on the soundness of their investor base, the extent to which their central bank can support the government paper market in the short run, their growth potential, and whether public debt is increasing or decreasing. The urgency of fiscal adjustment, therefore, is not the same for all countries. Second, public debt will become a problem only if the issue is ignored. There is still time for an orderly, gradual reduction in public debt ratios, avoiding shortcuts and focusing on a combination of growth-enhancing policies and a moderate degree of fiscal austerity. That said, procrastination is becoming more and more dangerous for some countries, especially in Europe, and there is no room for complacency for any country lest we are forced to revisit the lessons of centuries of economic history.

Too Much Public Debt Is Harmful, and We Have Too Much Now

Public debt in advanced economies, measured as a percentage of GDP, is high by historical standards, its average across countries having reached the second highest level since at least the late nineteenth century, and having done so in the absence of major wars. Rather, starting from an already high level in 2007, public debt-to-GDP ratios have surged as fiscal policy has been used to mute the effects of the 2008–09 global recession. In only a few countries have public debt-to-GDP ratios started to decline. In most they have stabilized at the record levels reached previously. In some, including the United States, they are still rising.

Historically, high public debt has often been associated with public debt rollover crises. Many argue that it is also associated with lower potential GDP growth, and I believe recent studies have confirmed this. Finally, high debt prevents using fiscal policy to support economic activity should another shock hit the economy.

However, while some European countries earlier in the decade did suffer major public debt crises, and while potential growth has indeed declined markedly since the recent public debt surge, the most obvious symptoms of a public debt overhang are not really apparent at the moment. Remarkably, interest rates on public debt, the most obvious signal of excessive debt accumulation, are still low, though they have been edging up recently. Why? Interest rates have been kept low by massive public debt monetization undertaken by central banks: a large part of the increase in public debt since the 2008–09 global recession was purchased by central banks. The surge in liquidity was motivated not so much by fiscal dominance (the subjugation of monetary policy to the needs of the government) but by the desire to raise the inflation rate, which has been undershooting targets for a while, and boost economic activity. Yet the liquidity surge helped facilitate the financing of government deficits and debt, giving the impression that we have entered a new era in which public debt is no longer a problem. Moreover, the monetary surge has not so far resulted in inflation (at least not consumer price inflation, though asset prices may have been affected) because banks have been willing to hold the increased liquidity idle in the central bank vaults, perhaps because of lack of demand for loans even at low interest rates, or perhaps, as I have argued, because they are constrained by lack of equity.

Why should we worry? We should worry because we are in uncharted waters: never has there been such a rapid rise in public debt except as a result of wars, and war economies work in quite different ways. And never has there been such a surge in the supply of liquidity by central banks in the absence of inflation. We should also worry because, unless we have entered a brave new world in which old economic laws no longer apply, economic history tells us that the current calm is unlikely to last forever. Banks will sooner or later start using their excess liquidity to make loans and, unless central banks mop it up rapidly, this will put pressure on prices, real interest rates, and the differential between interest rates and growth rates, which is what matters for the dynamics of the public debt-to-GDP ratio. That is when the lightness of public debt will morph into a heavy burden, perhaps unbearable for some countries.

So the current high-public-debt, low-interest-rates, low-inflation environment will not last forever, and stabilizing public debt at the current high levels would not be a good idea. Public debt needs to be brought down at a speed that depends on country circumstances, first and foremost countries' exposure to the risk of a rollover crisis. The issue is how to do it, as lowering public debt also involves some costs. Some shortcuts are, in principle, available. They hold the promise of lower costs, but they lead in the wrong direction.

Shortcuts Do Not Work, Are Costly, or Are Not Effective

We have considered various shortcuts. Debt repudiation has the advantage of being fast. It is like surgery, and there is no stepping back once it has been decided. However, like surgery, debt repudiation is risky and may have very high costs. The reputational costs are perhaps not as slight as some have argued, especially if large haircuts are needed. Most important, if public debt is held domestically, debt repudiation is equivalent to taxing some domestic residents, those who hold government paper, with related recessionary effects. Even when public debt is held abroad, the spillover effects for defaulting countries can be huge, especially if the defaulting countries are sizable. We need only consider the mess that resulted in European financial markets when a country as small as Greece decided to restructure its debt in late 2011.

Financial repression is a sort of crawling default and may be difficult to enforce. The kind of accidental financial repression that is currently resulting from tight equity regulations is helping finance governments, including by avoiding the immediate inflationary effects of the central bank financing of fiscal deficits, but will not last forever unless it is made more binding, which would be costly for the working of the economy.

Using monetary policy to inflate public debt away, and not just to stimulate the economy and bring inflation back to its 2 percent target, could work, but, to be decisive, would require an inflation outburst that would perhaps be difficult to keep under control. For many high-debt European countries this route would also require leaving the euro zone, something that, according to many, is a requirement for these countries to resume growing at faster rates, as exiting the euro zone would allow them to recover competitiveness. But the costs of a euro exit would be large, and I believe that the road of faster growth can be resumed more easily through structural reforms. This would not be impossible, though it does require political resolve.

Mutualizing public debt, at least for those countries that, in theory, would have this possibility, such as the euro-zone countries, would be nice, but it will not happen, as it would require a degree of economic altruism that is not present even in economic areas that have reached a political union, such as the federal states.

Finally, selling government assets could also work, if there were enough assets to sell. Unfortunately, this is not the case in today's advanced economies. Privatization revenues can support and accelerate the decline in the debt ratio, but the latter would have to be driven primarily by other forces.

The Main Road: Structural Reforms to Boost Potential Growth and a Moderate Degree of Fiscal Austerity

The road to bringing down public debt is a combination of growth-enhancing structural reforms and a moderate degree of fiscal austerity, leading to an orderly, gradual decline in the public debt ratio.

Raising the GDP growth rate would facilitate enormously the public debt reduction process, but there are several caveats. First, faster growth and a decline in debt cannot be achieved through a fiscal expansion, as some have argued: if you want to go in one direction you cannot start by moving in the opposite direction, or, as the old adage says, if you are in a hole, stop digging. What is needed is not a demand-driven temporary increase in the growth rate, which is what at best a fiscal expansion could generate, but a rise in the long-term growth rate of the economy. This requires structural reforms, whose content needs to be defined at the country level. However, structural reforms are difficult, require time to implement, and take even longer to yield results. Moreover, their effects cannot be precisely quantified. Altogether, it would not be credible to design a debt reduction plan based on optimistic expectations of high returns from growth-enhancing structural reforms. Finally, most of the effects of higher growth on the public debt ratio arise if the higher tax revenues associated with faster growth are, at least in part, saved by the government. In other words, some degree of fiscal austerity is need.

This brings me to the second pillar of the gradual public debt reduction strategy: a moderate degree of fiscal austerity. Growth, even the relatively modest growth that some high-debt countries are experiencing today, will bring in more revenues, and if primary public spending is not raised in line with GDP, the deficit will decline and debt accumulation will slow or be reversed. The specific degree of fiscal austerity, defined by the extent to which the rise in primary spending would be kept below the rise in GDP (or the degree to which revenues would be raised faster than GDP through tax increases, if a country preferred to act on the tax side rather than on the spending side), should depend on country circumstances. But even in high-debt countries a strategy of moderate austerity can work if it is pursued steadily and transparently.

In Italy, the country I discussed more closely in this book but whose situation is similar to that of other high-debt European countries where tax rates are already elevated (France, Portugal, and Spain, for example), my proposal would be to freeze primary government spending in real terms, for as long as it takes to balance the budget. Spending should only be allowed to rise in line with inflation. Balancing the budget is not always the right policy and, if followed forever, it would lead to a trend decline (toward zero) in the public debt-to-GDP ratio, which has no economic justification. But for a country with a public debt as high as Italy's and other European countries', it seems the reasonable thing to do, until public debt has fallen to more reassuring levels.

A balanced budget, for Italy and other European countries, would imply a steady decline in the public debt ratio, at a pace depending on the growth rate of the economy. Most likely it would take decades before public debt fell below the 60 percent threshold required by European rules and a reasonable long-term debt target. The process can be accelerated a bit by privatization revenues. But, most important, if the public debt ratio is declining at a sufficient speed (by, say, three to four percentage points per year), exposure to the risks and costs related to high public debt (the risks of a rollover crisis and lower potential growth) is likely to be more contained.

Reaching and maintaining a balanced budget is not inconsistent with continuing the growth process, in the short and the long run. The proposed freeze in real spending, to be maintained until the budget is balanced, would not subtract much from aggregate demand. Once the budget is balanced, primary spending could start rising again, in line with GDP. A balanced budget could be maintained in cyclically adjusted terms to allow the automatic stabilizers to operate, with deficits in weaker phases of the economic cycle offset by surpluses in stronger phases. Primary surpluses would have to be maintained at a higher level than in the past and in other economies, but in countries in which primary public spending is in the range of 45 to 50 percent of GDP, it should not be impossible to find areas where savings can be achieved without a major impact on the key public services provided to households and firms, and hence on potential growth. It may even help improve economic efficiency by removing distortions.

Outside Europe, the United States and Japan have also so far been unable to bring down their public debt levels from the peaks reached after the global crisis and have relied massively, especially Japan, on central bank financing. The United States still enjoys what has been called the "exorbitant privilege" of issuing the main reserve currency of the world, which means that central banks in other parts of the world invest heavily in securities issued by the U.S. government. In general, U.S. government paper is considered a safe haven for investors when financial markets are stressed. This is a big advantage. But the ability to issue a reserve currency is not something written in stone, and pressures from age-related spending will increase rapidly over the next decade, significantly weakening the U.S. fiscal accounts. So the United States has more time, but not an eternity of time, to put its fiscal house in order.

Japan needs to move more rapidly. The burden of public debt in Japan is not as high as its gross public debt-to-GDP ratio would suggest because of the high levels of its financial assets, the huge holdings of government debt by its central bank, and, in general, the low level of its public debt held by private foreign investors. But public debt keeps rising, and if Japanese banks started to diversify their portfolios, particularly by buying foreign assets, this could jeopardize financial stability in Japan and elsewhere. Japan's fiscal problems are just too big to be ignored.

The Need for Political Leadership

The current phase of low interest rates provides a breathing space in which to address the high public debt problem through a gradual process of public debt consolidation. Low rates will not last forever, and when the next financial market shock hits the world economy, countries that are not prepared will suffer heavily.

Unfortunately, low interest rates also remove the pressure to strengthen the fiscal accounts. Some countries manage to consolidate their accounts while interest rates are still relatively low. Canada in the 1990s is a good example. Others tend to act only when they are under pressure from the financial markets, which makes the adjustment more difficult because the economy shrinks as a result of both the rise in interest rates and the tightening of fiscal policy. That was the case of Italy in 2011–12. This scenario should be avoided. Implementing a debt reduction plan ultimately requires the recognition by the political system and the population at large that high public debt is bad for the economy. There is no need to demonize public debt. It is only when public debt is too much that it becomes harmful. But the issue of excessive public debt should not be trivialized either. High-debt countries still have time to fix the problem, and strengthening fiscal institutions and enhancing the transparency of the fiscal accounts will help foster the culture of fiscal rectitude that is needed to start lowering public debt and to sustain the effort over time. But time is running short, especially in Europe, where the process of reducing the public debt ratios can no longer be postponed. It will be a long process and should not be further delayed.

Will there be enough political leadership to guide this task? Skeptics say that politicians have too much to lose to implement fiscal adjustment and that those who have pursued fiscal adjustment in the past ended up being punished later by the electorate. However, the strategy of gradual fiscal adjustment that I propose is not inconsistent with maintaining a satisfactory growth pace, and it can work as long as it is not further delayed. Inaction, on the other hand, will end up in new rollover crises, and these crises usually do cause the collapse of governments. So politicians are not necessarily worse off by deciding not to delay fiscal adjustment. In any case, real leaders should not be guided by expectations about the outcome of the next elections but by ideals, and by the courage to pursue them. Solving the public debt problem needs that kind of leader, and those kinds of ideals.

Notes

Chapter 1

1. Public debt is not quite the sum of all previous deficits because some items, while contributing to a change in debt, are not included in the definition of deficit. For example, government debt may increase because the government is borrowing to build up its bank deposits (this borrowing is not part of the deficit because it is matched by an increase in assets). The discrepancies between the deficit and the change in debt are always worth looking at closely because sometimes governments use creative accounting to artificially reduce the deficit, while changes in public debt are more difficult to hide.

2. For simplicity, we will refer to general government debt as *public debt*. However, strictly speaking, in international public finance standards, the term "public debt" refers to a somewhat broader definition of government, encompassing public enterprises as well. In the United States, the term is used to indicate the debt issued by the federal government (see www.treasury.gov/resource-center/faqs/Markets /Pages/national-debt.aspx); more on this in chapter 2.

3. The duration of a government security takes into account not only when the security will have to be repaid but also how interest payments are distributed over time.

4. A higher risk will tend to increase the interest rate premium required by investors. This effect is at least partly offset by the fact that shorter maturities usually bear a lower interest rate because they are more liquid, with the uncertainty increasing for investments of longer maturity.

5. For the sake of completeness, I will mention a third form of debt, one not usually included in the official public debt statistics: payment arrears. When the public sector misses a payment, a payment arrear arises. The government owes money to the private sector and must pay interest on this debt. In some emerging countries, these arrears amount to several percentage points of GDP. As they are not included

in official debt statistics, when they are eventually paid by borrowing money from markets, the measured public debt increases.

Chapter 2

1. Longer time series on public debt available for the United Kingdom show that public debt in that country reached its historical peak in the early nineteenth century as a result of the Napoleonic Wars.

2. The support given to financial institutions usually implies the acquisition by the government of the intervened financial institutions, and, hence, the increase in the government financial assets. This is one of the reasons why net public debt (that is, gross debt netted out of the financial assets held by the government) increased a bit less (about thirty-two percentage points of GDP) than the gross debt figures reported in figure 2-1.

3. Various other figures for public debt are used for the United States (see the U.S. Treasury website at www.treasury.gov/resource-center/faqs/Markets/Pages /national-debt.aspx).

4. The corresponding dollar figures are available at www.treasurydirect.gov /govt/reports/pd/mspd/2015/opds122015.pdf.

5. This includes the *Time* magazine article by James Grant ("The United States of Insolvency") quoted in the introduction, which compared data for the United States referring to the federal government with the data of other countries referring to the whole general government.

6. The argument for looking at net debt is even stronger when the financial assets are the very securities issued by the central government. Some components of the general government, typically public pension funds, invest in government securities (again, this is particularly relevant for Japan and Canada). In other words, the public sector lends to and borrows from itself. In this respect, the data reported in figure 2-2, drawn from the IMF's *Fiscal Monitor* of October 2016, are not fully consistent because for some countries (European countries, the United States) they are already netted out of the holdings of government debt by other public entities, while for others (notably Japan and Canada) they are not.

7. These arguments for looking at gross rather than net figures hold even more strongly for real assets held by the government. Should they also not be netted out? Probably not, for most purposes. The yield from real assets (land, buildings) is much more difficult to assess; moreover, the liquidity of real assets is quite low, and so real assets do not really help alleviate the rollover problems that may arise in the government paper market. Real assets, however, could over time be used to repay public debt.

8. These figures are computed using a methodology similar to that used for computing pension debt, namely, by looking at the net present value of projected health spending increases between 2016 and 2050 (see table A23 of the IMF's *Fiscal Monitor,* October 2016, www.imf.org/external/pubs/ft/fm/2016/02/pdf/fm1602 .pdf).

9. See Congressional Budget Office, "The 2016 Long-Term Budget Outlook," July 12, 2016 (www.cbo.gov/publication/51580), and Committee for a Responsible Federal Budget, "The Very, Very Long-Term Budget Outlook," July 19, 2016 (http://crfb.org/blogs/very-very-long-term-budget-outlook).

10. See, for example, Larry Summers, "The Age of Secular Stagnation: What It Is and What to Do about It," *Foreign Affairs*, February 15, 2016 (http://larrysummers.com/2016/02/17/the-age-of-secular-stagnation/).

11. The injection of liquidity ("money") in the economy by central banks should stimulate an increase in commercial bank credit. When central banks buy government securities from banks, the latter's deposits at the central bank increase. As these deposits yield no interest (or may even bear a negative interest rate), commercial banks should try to use this added liquidity to lend to their customers by lowering the interest rates on their commercial loans, including, for example, mortgages, which should stimulate the economy.

Chapter 3

1. More details on Ponzi's scheme are available in the excellent biography by Mitchell Zuckoff, *Ponzi's Scheme: The True Story of a Financial Legend* (New York: Random House, 2006).

2. In defining the criterion for debt sustainability, I moved from what economists call the "no-Ponzi-game condition" (that is, the fact that the government is not running a Ponzi scheme) to a somewhat different condition, namely, the stability of the public debt-to-GDP ratio. These conditions are similar but not exactly equivalent. Respecting the no-Ponzi-game condition technically requires that the present value of the sum of future primary surpluses be at least equal to the current value of public debt. It can be shown that, as long as the average interest rate on public debt is higher than the GDP growth rate, this condition is met if the public debt-to-GDP ratio is stable over time. However, if the GDP growth rate is higher than the interest rate on public debt—as happens in many countries, especially in many emerging countries—the public debt-to-GDP ratio may be stable even when the no-Ponzi-game condition is not met: when this happens, a country can maintain over time a constant debt ratio even if it runs primary deficits. However, the stability of the debt ratio is still regarded by most economists as a sufficient indicator of government solvency because GDP is a sort of "guarantee" of the possibility of the government servicing its debt (economists say that in this case, the government is running an "honest Ponzi scheme"). These more technical issues are discussed in Leonardo Bartolini and Carlo Cottarelli, "Government Ponzi Games and the Sustainability of Public Deficits under Uncertainty," *Ricerche Economiche* 48, no. 1 (1994), pp. 1–22.

Chapter 4

1. In an open economy, imports would also rise, but this is an unnecessary complication for our purposes.

2. This episode is reported in the book *The Coming of Keynesianism to America: Conversations with the Founders of Keynesian Economics*, edited by David C. Colander and Harry Landreth (Cheltenham, U.K.: Edward Elgar, 1996), p. 109. However, according to Alvin Hansen, whose views are reported in the same book, "Keynes was never interested in the national debt: he never really gave any serious systematic discussion, as far as I can remember, to the debt" (p. 105). Readers interested in this issue can refer to a study by Tony Aspromourgos, "Keynes, Lerner and the Question of Public Debt," *History of Political Economy* 46, no. 3 (2014), pp. 409–33.

3. See Nancy Churchman, *David Ricardo on Public Debt* (Basingstoke, U.K.: Palgrave Macmillan, 2001).

4. See Danielle Kurtzleben, "National Debt Interest Payments Dwarf Other Government Spending," *U.S. News and World Report*, November 19, 2012 (www.usnews.com/news/articles/2012/11/19/how-the-nations-interest-spending-stacks-up). See also the article by Maya MacGuineas, president of the nonpartisan Committee for a Responsible Federal Budget, "The First Step: Stop Digging," *Washington Post*, September 2, 2016.

5. Models of this kind are included, for example, in Olivier J. Blanchard, "Current and Anticipated Deficits, Interest Rates and Economic Activity," Working Paper 1265 (Cambridge, Mass.: National Bureau of Economic Research, January 1984) (www.nber.org/papers/w1265.pdf). Note that in some economic models the interest rate prevailing in the economy depends not on public debt but on the fiscal deficit. It does not make much difference. Given a certain growth rate of nominal GDP, there is a long-term stable relationship between the public debt-to-GDP ratio and the fiscal deficit-to-GDP ratio in the sense that if the latter is stable, the former is also stable. For example, for a given growth rate of GDP of 3.5 percent, a fiscal deficit ratio of 4 percent implies (and leads to) a public debt ratio of 120 percent, while a fiscal deficit ratio of 2 percent implies a public debt ratio of 60 percent in the long run.

6. Remarks by Chairman Alan Greenspan before the Bond Market Association, White Sulphur Springs, West Virginia (via videoconference), April 27, 2001 (www.federalreserve.gov/boardDocs/speeches/2001/20010427/default.htm).

7. Ken Rogoff and Carmen Reinhart, "Growth in a Time of Debt," Working Paper 15639 (Cambridge, Mass.: National Bureau of Economic Research, January 2010) (www.nber.org/papers/w15639).

8. A list of the papers that show that high public debt lowers potential growth can be found in a paper I wrote with Laura Jaramillo, "Walking Hand in Hand: Fiscal Policy and Growth in Advanced Economies," Working Paper 12/137 (Washington, D.C.: International Monetary Fund, May 2012) (www.imf.org/external/pubs/ft/wp/2012/wp12137.pdf). To be fair, there is also a paper by Ugo Panizza and Andrea F. Presbitero, "Public Debt and Economic Growth: Is there a Causal Effect?," Working Paper 65 (Geneva: Money and Finance Working Group, and Centre for Macroeconomic and Finance Research, April 2012) (https://ideas.repec.org/p/anc/wmofir/65.html), that does not find conclusive evidence of a negative effect of higher debt on potential growth.

9. Manmohan S. Kumar and Jaejoon Woo, "Public Debt and Growth," Working Paper 10/174 (Washington, D.C.: International Monetary Fund, July 2010) (www .imf.org/external/pubs/ft/wp/2010/wp10174.pdf).

10. Andrea Pescatori, Damiano Sandri, and John Simon, "Debt and Growth: Is There a Magic Threshold?," Working Paper 14/34 (Washington, D.C.: International Monetary Fund, February 2014) (www.imf.org/external/pubs/ft/wp/2014/wp1434 .pdf).

Chapter 5

1. Franklin D. Roosevelt, address to the American Retail Federation, Washington, D.C., May 22, 1939.

2. The similarity of the words for debt and guilt in German is noted by David Graeber in *Debt: The First 5,000 Years* (New York: Melville House, 2011), esp. pp. 56–57 and 77. Graeber also notes that the German philosopher Friedrich Nietzsche had already underscored the implications of that similarity. However, Graeber notes that a common root for the words "debt," "sin," and "guilt" exists in other European languages as well (p. 120) and has been identified in the earliest written documents, such as the Vedic poems of the second millennium BC.

3. As noted by Simon Johnson and James Kwak in their excellent book on public debt in the United States, *White House Burning: Our National Debt and Why It Matters to You* (New York: Vintage Books, 2013), "The moralistic attitude—not dispassionate analysis of the costs and benefits of borrowing—has shaped public rhetoric about the federal government's finances for most of American history" (p. 135).

4. The apocryphal nature of this quote is documented at http://quoteinvestigator .com/2-13/05/15/cicero-budget/. For references to politicians using Cicero's fake quote, see www.snopes.com/quotes/cicero.asp.

5. The text of the speeches was reprinted in *Enrico Berlinguer: L'austerità giusta* [Enrico Berlinguer: The fair austerity], edited by Giulio Marcon (Milan: Jaka Book, 2014).

Chapter 7

1. Years ago I studied the relationship between inflation and fiscal policy in a paper written with two IMF colleagues. See Carlo Cottarelli, Mark E. L. Griffiths, and Reza Moghadam, "The Nonmonetary Determinants of Inflation: A Panel Data Study," Working Paper 98/23 (Washington, D.C.: International Monetary Fund, March 1998) (http://papers.ssrn.com/sol3/papers.cfm?abstract_id=882254).

2. There are other ways inflation can improve the fiscal accounts. For example, if spending is fixed in nominal terms, inflation can reduce the deficit itself, as incomes and revenues rise when there is inflation. But this is likely to be a short-term effect as spending would soon be adjusted. Also, more inflation increases the amount of money the economy needs, and hence seigniorage. But in modern economies the

most important channel is the one discussed in the text (namely, the erosion of the real value of the bonds in circulation).

3. The results are summarized in the IMF's *Fiscal Monitor* of April 2013 (www .imf.org/en/Publications/FM/Issues/2016/12/31/Fiscal-Adjustment-in-an -Uncertain-World), esp. pp. 30–31.

Chapter 8

1. See Paul De Grauwe and Yuemei Ji, "Self-Fulfilling Crises in the Eurozone: An Empirical Test," CEPS Working Document 367 (Belgium: Centre for European Policy Studies, June 2012) (www.ceps.eu/system/files/WD%20No%20367%20 Empirical%20Test%20Fragility%20Eurozone.pdf).

2. The theory of optimal currency areas was introduced in Robert A. Mundell, "A Theory of Optimum Currency Areas," *American Economic Review* 51, no. 4 (1961), pp. 657–65 (assets.aeaweb.org/assets/production/journals/aer/top20/51.4.657 -665.pdf). Many believe that Mundell's paper argues that a common currency in Europe would have no future. Actually, Mundell said that the feasibility of a European currency would depend on whether, empirically, labor (and capital) mobility would be sufficiently high. Mundell was much more trenchant in concluding that Canada, his own country, was not an optimal currency area. In other words, Mundell had predicted that the Canadian dollar had no future.

3. *Annual Report of the Bank of Italy*, final remarks of the governor, May 1998 (my translation).

4. The gap is larger including the 2009–14 period, but this is because the 2011–12 euro-zone crisis hit Italy more severely and caused a decline in output that, hopefully, has a temporary component.

5. In more technical terms, the real appreciation of the unit labor cost effective exchange rate could be corrected either through a nominal depreciation or through an "internal devaluation," that is, by keeping wage growth below productivity growth. The effects in terms of real wages would be the same, though. The two routes, nominal depreciation and internal devaluation, are not, however, exactly identical. Internal devaluation leads to deflation and, if this lowers inflation expectations, real interest rates will increase, which will lower aggregate demand. This would reduce the beneficial effect on growth of the recovery in competitiveness, which would require, in general, more expansive policies in the euro zone as a whole, as argued in a recent paper by IMF staff: Jörg Decressin and others, "Wage Moderation in Crises: Policy Considerations and Applications to the Euro Area," IMF Staff Discussion Note 15/22, November 2015 (www.imf.org/external/pubs/ft/sdn/2015/sdn1522.pdf). This problem, however, would arise only if inflation expectations change as a result of what should be a one-off correction in domestic wages.

6. See "UBS: Euro Break-up: The Consequences," CreditWritedowns.com, September 6, 2011 (www.creditwritedowns.com/2011/09/eurozone-breakup-consequences .html).

7. Alberto Bagnai, *Il tramonto dell'euro* [The sunset of the euro] (Reggio Emilia: Imprimatur Editore, 2012).

8. Some, including Alberto Bagnai in *Il tramonto dell'euro* (p. 346), argue that a change in the currency denomination of public debt (from the euro to the new lira) would not be regarded as a case of default. However, in international practice, any change in the terms of the contract, including conversion into a new currency, would likely be regarded as a default. Sometimes one hears about the possibility that the currency conversion of a G-7 country (such as Italy) would not be regarded as a default because of a provision included in the definitions of default of the International Swap and Derivatives Association. That provision did exist but was changed in 2014. I did some digging, and it seems likely that, under the new definition, a currency conversion by any country would constitute default (at a minimum, it would give rise to complex litigation). In any case, the economic reality is that a redenomination into a currency subject to fast depreciation would lead to a loss for bondholders similar to the one they would suffer in the case of outright default.

9. I have not discussed another reason why euro-skeptics believe that leaving the euro zone would revive growth and in this way help resolve fiscal problems, namely, the fact that leaving the euro zone would free countries from the constraints imposed by the ironclad fiscal rules of the euro zone. These rules, which are not so ironclad, are discussed in chapter 16.

Chapter 9

1. Carmen M. Reinhart and M. Belen Sbrancia, "The Liquidation of Government Debt," Working Paper 16893 (Cambridge, Mass.: National Bureau of Economic Research, 2011) (www.imf.org/external/np/seminars/eng/2011/res2/pdf/crbs .pdf).

2. The Indian government not only has a deficit, it also has a primary deficit: spending exceeds revenues even when interest payments are netted out. So do many other emerging economies, often with the help of financial repression.

3. A tightening of bank regulations in today's world is much more effective if it is undertaken in a coordinated way, as otherwise banks could move their activities, at least in part, to countries with less stringent bank rules.

4. One of the reasons why low interest rates reduce the profitability of banks is that interest rates on deposits cannot become negative (otherwise depositors would ask for their money back, as banknotes yield at least a zero interest rate, and a zero yield is better than a negative yield). So if interest rates on bank assets decline, and banks cannot lower their deposit rates below zero, bank profits shrink.

Chapter 10

1. The quotation opens Graeber's bestseller *Debt: The First 5,000 Years* (New York: Melville House, 2011), p. 2.

2. The terms of the contract under which government securities are issued (defining, for example, the modalities of their repayment) are included in a *prospectus*, a formal legal document issued under the law of a given country.

3. Carmen M. Reinhart and Kenneth Rogoff, *This Time Is Different: Eight Centuries of Financial Folly* (Princeton University Press, 2009), p. 320.

4. In addition to Greece, Portugal and Ireland are sometimes also cited as cases of recent debt restructuring in advanced economies, but in these two countries the debt restructuring was more formal than substantive. What happened is that Portugal and Ireland also benefited from being extended the better terms on which European countries and institutions decided to lend to Greece.

5. Lachman argues that it is very uncertain whether Italy, Ireland, and Portugal will manage to maintain a primary surplus at a sufficiently high level for sufficiently long enough to lower public debt to sustainable levels (*Financial Times*, January 8, 2015); Mody calls for a "Uruguay-style" debt restructuring, meaning a lengthening of maturities ("It's True, Italy Breaks Your Heart," *The Bruegel Newsletter*, October 10, 2014 [http:bruegel.org/2014/10/its-true-italy-breaks-your-heart/]). For Willem Buiter's contribution, see "The Debt of Nations: Prospects for Debt Restructuring by Sovereigns and Banks in Advanced Economies," *CFA Institute Conference Proceedings Quarterly* 28, no. 3 (September 2011) (www.cfainstitute.org/learning /products/publications/cp/Pages/cp.v28.n3.10.aspx).

6. Peter Boone and Simon Johnson, "The European Crisis Deepens," Policy Brief PB12-4 (Washington, D.C.: Peterson Institute for International Economics, 2012); Bouriel Roubini, "Time to Act: Italy Must Restructure Its Debt," *Financial Times*, November 29, 2011.

7. Eduardo Borensztein and Ugo Panizza, "The Costs of Sovereign Default," Working Paper 03/238 (Washington, D.C.: International Monetary Fund, October 2008) (www.imf.org/external/pubs/ft/wp/2008/wp08238.pdf).

8. Juan J. Cruces and Christopher Trebesch, "Sovereign Defaults: The Price of Haircuts," *American Economic Journal* 5, no. 3 (2013), pp. 85–117.

9. Debt restructuring usually also requires some traditional form of fiscal adjustment. If a country has a primary deficit it would have to eliminate that primary deficit by raising (regular) taxes or cutting spending, even if debt were completely canceled. Indeed, after defaulting on public debt, a country will probably be unable, at least for some time, to borrow in the financial markets, which requires running a balanced budget, even assuming all debt is canceled, which is very unlikely. Most of the time, countries find it difficult to apply a 100 percent haircut, so some debt will continue to be serviced, which will require running a primary surplus.

10. In the case of Italy, Francesco Lippi and Fabiano Schivardi have noted, in "Le conseguenze di un ripudio: Del debito" [The consequences of dept repudiation], lavoce.info, May 16, 2014 (www.lavoce.info/archives/19664/conseguenze-ripudio -debito/), that Italian banks would end up being severely undercapitalized in the event of a restructuring of government debt.

11. As discussed in the next chapter, this is exactly what happened in the case of the Greek debt restructuring: banks had to be sheltered, which significantly reduced the impact of the restructuring on the public debt-to-GDP ratio.

12. Adair Turner, *Between Debt and the Devil: Money, Credit, and Fixing Global Finance* (Princeton University Press, 2015), p. 226.

13. A detailed description of this policy is available at www.imf.org/external/np /exr/facts/privsec.htm.

14. The IMF's document on how to assess public debt sustainability can be found at www.imf.org/en/publications/policy-papers/issues/2016/12/31/staff-guidance-note -for-public-debt-sustainability-analysis-in-market-access-countries-pp4771.

Chapter 11

1. I say this with some regret: the loss of confidence in the German rectitude caused by the Volkswagen scandal makes sorry anyone, like me, who saw Germany as an example for other countries.

Chapter 12

1. Almost all common currency areas are also political unions. The comparison here is with federal states because they are the least intensive form of political union and therefore are more easily comparable with the European Union, which is an even less intensive form of political union.

2. The IMF proposal can be found at https://www.imf.org/external/pubs/ft/sdn /2013/sdn1309tn.pdf.

3. This point is discussed in more detail in chapter 2 of Carlo Cottarelli and Martine Guerguil, eds., *Designing a European Fiscal Union: Lessons from the Experience of Fiscal Federations* (New York: Routledge, 2015).

4. A proposal by the Italian minister of finance, Pier Carlo Padoan, to centralize some EU fiscal policies can be found in his "Italia propone un Fondo Salva-Lavoro per i Paesi dell'area euro" [Italy proposes a fund to boost employment in euro zone countries] (Ministry of the Economy and Finance, October 6, 2015) (www.mef.gov .it/inevidenza/article_0165.html).

5. A summary of all these proposals is available at https://www.imf.org/external /pubs/ft/wp/2012/wp12172.pdf.

6. A proposal including the provision of real guarantees was put forward, for example, by former Italian prime minister Romano Prodi and Alberto Quadrio Curzio in a letter to the Italian financial newspaper *Sole-24 Ore* on August 23, 2011.

7. One exception is Austria, where the central government borrows from financial markets to lend to members of the Austrian federation. But this is the exception, not the rule. This issue is discussed in chapter 5 of Cottarelli and Guerguil, *Designing a European Fiscal Union*.

8. For a detailed description on the debate over U.S. public debt in the aftermath of the war of independence, the reader can refer to chapter 1 of Simon Johnson and

James Kwak, *White House Burning: Our National Debt and Why It Matters to You* (New York: Random House, 2012).

9. See the excellent paper (not available in English) by Floriana Cerniglia, "Stato unitario, ragioni politiche e regole economiche: Il divario regionale nello Stato unitario dal 1861 al 1887," [Unitary state, political considerations, and economic rules: The regional gap in the unitary state from 1861 to 1887], *Annali di Storia Moderna e Contemporanea* 1 (1995).

10. Pierre Pâris and Charles Wyplosz, "The PADRE Plan: Politically Acceptable Debt Restructuring in the Eurozone" (London: Centre for Economic Policy Research, January 28, 2014) (http://voxeu.org/article/padre-plan-politically-acceptable-debt-restructuring-eurozone).

Chapter 13

1. Niall Ferguson, *The Cash Nexus: Money and Power in the Modern World, 1700–2000* (New York: Basic Books, 2001).

2. Yogi Berra, the baseball player famous for his sometimes naïve but effective aphorisms, does not really seem to have said anything about the difference between theory and practice, but the sentence in the epigraph is nevertheless often included among Yogiberrisms.

3. Aspects of the United Kingdom's Whole of Government accounts can be found at www.nao.org.uk/highlights/whole-of-government-accounts.

Chapter 14

1. A 43 percent tax ratio is close to the one prevailing in Italy in 2015.

2. If you feel like it, you can compute the figures yourself, but otherwise trust me.

3. S. Ali Abbas and others, "A Historical Public Debt Database," Working Paper 10/245 (Washington, D.C.: International Monetary Fund, November 2010) (www.imf.org/external/pubs/ft/wp/2010/wp10245.pdf).

4. See Niall Ferguson, *The Cash Nexus: Money and Power in the Modern World, 1700–2000* (New York; Basic Books, 2001), pp. 121–123.

5. There have been endless controversies over the value of the fiscal multiplier, how it differs across kinds of spending, to what extent it is different in case of tax cuts or spending increases, and how much it is affected by whether the additional government deficit is financed by borrowing from the public or borrowing from the central bank (that is, by printing money), by the magnitude of the spare capacity in the economy, or by the size of public debt, among other things. A value of 1 would be seen as high by some and low by others (the very term "multiplier" comes from the idea that deficit spending would increase demand by a multiple, so multiplying by 1 is not much of a multiplication!). I take the multiplier to be 1 for illustrative purposes, but it is not too far from what many economists would regard as a sensible figure. In any case, the higher the multiplier, the more beneficial would be an increase in public spending for GDP and the public debt ratio.

6. The reader may have noted that the initial decline in the debt-to-GDP ratio results from the fact that the public debt ratio is quite high in this example. It is an arithmetic fact that a ratio increases or declines depending on whether the percentage change in its numerator is higher or lower than the percentage change in its denominator. The percentage change in the denominator (GDP) would be the same for all countries with an initial GDP level of 1,000. But the percentage change in the numerator would depend on the initial debt level. If a country has a high debt level, adding $12 to it implies a small percentage increase in debt, and hence the debt ratio may decline, as in the example.

7. A version of this story is available in J. Bradford DeLong and Lawrence H. Summers, "Fiscal Policy in a Depressed Economy" (Brookings Institution, Spring 2012) (www.brookings.edu/bpea-articles/fiscal-policy-in-a-depressed-economy/).

8. Vitor Gaspar, Maurice Obstfeld, and Ratna Sahay, "Macroeconomic Management When Policy Space Is Constrained: A Comprehensive, Consistent and Coordinated Approach to Economic Policy," Staff Discussion Notes 16/09 (Washington, D.C.: International Monetary Fund, September 28, 2016) (www.imf.org/external/pubs/ft/sdn /2016/sdn1609.pdf), p. 10.

9. See, for example, Era Dabla-Norris and others, "Anchoring Growth: The Importance of Productivity-Enhancing Reforms in Emerging Markets and Developing Economies," *Journal of International Commerce, Economics and Policy* 5, no. 2 (2014) (http://dx.doi.org/10.1142/S179399331450001X).

10. Lawrence H. Summers, "U.S. Economic Prospects: Secular Stagnation, Hysteresis, and the Zero Lower Bound," *Business Economics* 49, no. 2 (2014), pp. 65–73.

11. Ignazio Visco, *Perché i tempi stanno cambiando* [Why the times are a-changing] (Bologna: Il Mulino, 2015), p. 26.

12. See Robert J. Gordon, *The Rise and Fall of American Growth: The U.S. Standard of Living since the Civil* War (Princeton University Press, 2016); and Erik Brynjolfsson and Andrew McAfee, *The Second Machine Age: Work: Progress, and Prosperity in a Time of Brilliant Technologies* (New York: Norton, 2016).

13. Thomas Piketty, *Capital in the Twenty-First Century*, translated by Arthur Goldhammer (Harvard University Press, 2014).

14. Atif Mian and Amir Sufi, *House of Debt: How They (and You) Caused the Great Recession, and How We Can Prevent It from Happening Again* (University of Chicago Press, 2014).

15. Raghuram G.Rajan, *Fault Lines: How Hidden Fractures Still Threaten the World Economy* (Princeton University Press, 2010).

16. See Manmohan S. Kumar and Jaejoon Woo, "Public Debt and Growth," Working Paper 10/174 (Washington, D.C.: International Monetary Fund, July 2010) (www.imf.org/external/pubs/ft/wp/2010/wp10174.pdf).

Chapter 15

1. See Carlo Cottarelli, *Il macigno: Perché il debito publico ci schiaccia e come si fa a liberarsene* [The boulder: Why public debt is crushing us, and how to get rid of it] (Milan: Feltrinelli, 2016).

2. Balancing the budget implies that the public debt-to-GDP ratio tends to fall to zero in the long run in relation to GDP. There is no strong economic reason why the public debt-to-GDP ratio should fall to zero in the long run, so a balanced budget may not be a good rule for the very long run. But I would not worry about this in a country that starts with a debt ratio above 130 percent. Moreover, aiming at a balanced budget would allow accommodating large noncyclical shocks, such as large and prolonged recessions, which may not be easily reversed.

3. In the lingo of fiscal economists, the terms "cyclically adjusted" and "structural" are not exactly equivalent. The former is used to refer to the correction for cyclical developments in GDP already mentioned in the previous section, while the latter includes corrections not only for cyclical forces but also for other temporary ("one-off") factors. We can ignore this distinction here.

4. Raphael Espinoza, Atish R. Ghosh, and Jonathan D. Ostry, "When Should Public Debt Be Reduced?," Staff Discussion Note 15/10 (Washington, D.C.: International Monetary Fund, June 2015) (www.imf.org/external/pubs/ft/sdn/2015/sdn1510.pdf).

5. The following analysis is based on the data collected for the book edited by Paulo Mauro, *Chipping Away at Public Debt: Sources of Failure and Keys to Success in Fiscal Adjustment* (Hoboken, N.J.: Wiley, 2011).

6. Indeed, a transfer is like a negative tax so, as a first approximation, it would have the same impact on demand.

7. See the IMF's *Fiscal Monitor* of October 2013, box 6 (www.imf.org/en /Publications/FM/Issues/2016/12/31/Taxing-Times).

Chapter 16

1. The IMF has collected information on fiscal rules around the world. The study was issued in December 2009 ("Fiscal Rules: Anchoring Expectations for Sustainable Public Finances" [Washington, D.C.: International Monetary Fund, December 16, 2009] [www.imf.org/external/np/pp/eng/2009/121609.pdf]) but the related data bank was updated more recently.

2. For Stiglitz, see Malcolm Moore, "Stiglitz Says European Austerity Plans Are a 'Suicide Pact,'" *The Telegraph*, January 17, 2012 (www.telegraph.co.uk/finance /financialcrisis/9019819/Stiglitz-says-European-austerity-plans-are-a-suicide-pact .html). For Krugman, see Paul Krugman, "Europe's Economic Suicide," op-ed, *New York Times*, April 15, 2012 (www.nytimes.com/2012/04/16/opinion/krugman-europes -economic-suicide.html).

3. Alexis Tsipras, "End Austerity before Fear Kills Greek Democracy," *Financial Times*, January 20, 2015 (www.ft.com/content/da236d24-9ff9-11e4-9a74-00144 feab7de).

4. European Commission, "Vade Mecum on the Stability and Growth Pact: 2016 Edition," Institutional Paper 21 (Brussels, March 23, 2016) (http://ec.europa.eu /economy_finance/publications/eeip/pdf/ip021_en.pdf).

5. More specifically, it was clarified that a country should reduce by one-twentieth every year the amount of the public debt-to-GDP ratio that exceeded

60 percent. This rule is often misunderstood. Some believe that the excess deficit to be reduced by one-twentieth every year is the one existing at the time when the rule was introduced, which would imply that the excess would be eliminated in twenty years. This interpretation may have made sense, but it is not what the rule says. The excess is recalculated every year, so that, for a country with a declining debt ratio, the required adjustment becomes lower and lower every year: the 60 percent debt level would be reached only asymptotically. Second, some believe the rule requires the deficit, not the debt, to decline by a certain amount every year, a serious misunderstanding. Others believe that public debt needs to decline in euro terms, while it just needs to decline as a percentage of GDP. The details of the debt rule are more complicated than I have laid out. For example, compliance with the rule has to be assessed in a forward-looking way, on a three-year average, thus taking into account a future reduction in the debt ratio that may not materialize in practice. Another element of flexibility is that, in assessing whether an insufficient pace of debt reduction could lead to sanctions, cyclical economic conditions are to be taken into account (the rule itself, however, focuses on the debt ratio unadjusted for cyclical conditions).

6. For example, each country's medium-term deficit objective is defined in structural terms, that is, by correcting for the economic cycle as well as for other temporary factors. The speed at which the deficit has to be corrected if it exceeds 3 percent is also to be assessed in structural terms. This flexibility is in practice reduced considerably for some countries because of the way the correction for the economic cycle is computed. The correction aims at identifying whether a country needs a larger deficit because its GDP is growing faster than normal. The normal pace, however, is considered to be very low for some countries. For example, in the last few years Italy and Portugal were believed to have a "normal" GDP growth rate of about zero. This meant that any positive growth was regarded, according to the European rules, as an economic boom, and the deficit had to be reduced at a pace faster than normal. See my note, "Potential Growth Rates and the Working of SGP Fiscal Rules" (Brussels: Centre for Economic Policy Research, March 2, 2015) (voxeu.org /article/assessing-compliance-stability-and-growth-pact-s-rules).

7. See, for example, Erif Arbatli and Julio Escolano, "Fiscal Transparency, Fiscal Performance and Credit Ratings," Working Paper 12/156 (Washington, D.C.: International Monetary Fund, June 2012) (www.imf.org/external/pubs/ft/wp/2012/wp12156 .pdf).

8. Xavier Debrun and IMF staff, "The Functions and Impact of Fiscal Councils" (Washington, D.C.: International Monetary Fund, July 16, 2013) (www.imf.org /external/np/pp/eng/2013/071613.pdf).

Index